Spheres of Injustice

This book presents a comprehensive overview of modern conceptualizations of justice in India. It analyses how these concepts relate to traditional theories of justice – in Marx, Ambedkar, Gandhi and Rawls as well as social realities in India.

The book critically analyses theories of justice in India from a theoretical and comparative framework. It brings together contributions by well-known scholars to explore a range of questions and dilemmas around justice which have been brought about by a widening disparity between the powerful and the marginalized. The volume engages with the inadequacies of tautological theories of justice and fairness which fall short of adequately articulating the institutionalized forms of injustices and inequality facing citizens in modern society. It also explores exceptions and deviations from transcendental and universalist assumptions of contemporary theories of justice and studies movements and expressions of dissent and alternative structures and paradigms of conceptualizing justice.

This book will be useful for scholars and researchers of political theory, political sociology, political studies, sociology, social theory, post-colonial theory and exclusion studies.

Albeena Shakil is Professor of English at O.P. Jindal Global University, Sonipat, Haryana. She has authored *Understanding the Novel: A Theoretical Overview*, 2015, and guest edited three issues of *Summerhill: IIAS Review*, IIAS Shimla. She also co-edited *JGLR: Women, Law and South Asia* (Upasana Mahanta and Sameena Dalwai), 2019.

Gopal Guru is Former Professor at Jawaharlal Nehru University, New Delhi. Currently he is the editor of *Economic and Political Weekly*. His published books include *Humiliation: Claims and Context* (Ed.), 2009; *The Cracked Mirror: An Indian Debate on Theory and Experience* (co-author Sundar Sarukkai), 2012; *Experience, Caste and the Everyday Social* (with Sundar Sarukkai), 2019. He has worked on Bhimrao Ambedkar's 'Philosophy of Moral Realism and Political Phenomenology of Touch' and contributed 'On Caste' in the *International Encyclopaedia of Anthropology*.

Spheres of Injustice

Edited by Albeena Shakil
and Gopal Guru

Routledge
Taylor & Francis Group

LONDON AND NEW YORK

Designed cover image: © Getty Images

First published 2023
by Routledge
4 Park Square, Milton Park, Abingdon, Oxon OX14 4RN

and by Routledge
605 Third Avenue, New York, NY 10158

Routledge is an imprint of the Taylor & Francis Group, an informa business

British Library Cataloguing-in-Publication Data
A catalogue record for this book is available from the British Library

ISBN: 978-0-367-40406-2 (hbk)
ISBN: 978-0-367-40408-6 (pbk)
ISBN: 978-0-429-35597-4 (ebk)

DOI: 10.4324/9780429355974

Typeset in Sabon
by Deanta Global Publishing Services, Chennai, India

Contents

Contributors

Samir Banerjee has been involved in activities related to development and change in many parts of the country, Tamil Nadu, Odisha, Madhya Pradesh, Andhra Pradesh, Maharashtra and Karnataka. This involvement has been with non-formal and non-governmental sector participants on issues ranging from appropriate technology to environment, slum habitats to non-formal education, sustainable development, watershed development, organic farming and informal studies regarding processes of social transformation and transition. These studies have spread over environment, organic farming, adult education and Gandhian Thought and its significance. His most recent book is *Tracing Gandhi: Satyarthi to Satyagrahi*, 2020.

Partha Chatterjee is Professor Emeritus of Anthropology and of Middle Eastern, South Asian and African Studies at Columbia University, New York, and Honorary Professor at the Centre for Studies in Social Sciences, Calcutta. He is a political theorist, political anthropologist and historian. He graduated from Presidency College, Calcutta, and received his PhD from the University of Rochester. Since 1997, he has divided his time between Columbia University and the Centre for Studies in Social Sciences, Calcutta, where he was the director from 1997 to 2007. He is the author of more than 30 books and edited volumes in English and Bengali. He was a founding member of the Subaltern Studies Collective. His books include *The Black Hole of Empire* (2012), *Lineages of Political Society* (2011), *Politics of the Governed* (2004), *A Princely Impostor? The Strange and Universal History of the Kumar of Bhawal* (2002), *The Nation and Its Fragments* (1993) and *Nationalist Thought and the Colonial World* (1986). He delivered the Ruth Benedict lectures in April 2018 which were published in an expanded version as *I Am the People: Reflections on Popular Sovereignty Today* (2019). His most recent book is an edition of a found manuscript entitled *The Truths and Lies of Nationalism as Narrated by Charvak* (2021).

Sobhanlal Datta Gupta is Former Surendra Nath Banerjee Professor of Political Science, University of Calcutta. He has primarily worked in the fields of political theory, Left politics in India and is currently engaged in exploring the intellectual history of an alternative Marxism. He is currently Honorary Co-Chair at the International Rosa Luxemburg Society (Berlin, Germany). Some of his recent publications include *Marxism in Dark Times: Select Essays for the New Century* (2012), *The Socialist Vision and the Silenced Voices of Democracy. Part I: Rosa Luxemburg* (2015), *Part II: Nikolai Bukharin* (2019).

Gopal Guru is Former Professor at Jawaharlal Nehru University, New Delhi. His published books include *Humiliation: Claims and Context*, Ed., 2009: *The Cracked Mirror: An Indian Debate on Theory and Experience* (co-author: Sundar Sarukkai) 2012; *Experience, Caste and the Everyday Social* (with Sundar Sarukkai) 2019. He has worked on Bhimrao Ambedkar's Philosophy of Moral Realism and Political Phenomenology of Touch and contributed On Caste in the *International Encyclopaedia of Anthropology*.

Gurpreet Mahajan teaches Political Philosophy at the Centre for Political Studies, Jawaharlal Nehru University. Her writings cover a range of subjects, from issues related to hermeneutic method and philosophy to questions of difference and discrimination in liberal democracies. Her publications include *Explanation and Understanding in the Human Sciences* (1992; 1997; 2011), *Identities and Rights: Aspects of Liberal Democracy in India* (1998), *The Multicultural Path: Issues of Diversity and Discrimination in Democracy* (Sage 2002) and *India: Political Ideas and the Making of a Democratic Discourse* (2013).

Sanjeeb Mukherjee is an independent researcher. He studied Politics at Presidency College and the University of Calcutta and received his PhD from the Department of Philosophy, Jadavpur University. He has held faculty positions in the Centre for Studies in Social Sciences, Calcutta, CSDS, Delhi, and the University of Calcutta and has lectured in universities in Norway, Sweden and England. His research and publications are in political theory, Indian politics and West Bengal.

Sundar Sarukkai works primarily in the philosophy of the natural and the social sciences. He is the founder of Barefoot Philosophers (www.barefootphilosophers.org). He is currently Visiting Faculty at the Centre for Society and Policy, Indian Institute of Science, Bangalore, India. He is the author of *Translating the World: Science and Language, Philosophy of Symmetry, Indian Philosophy and Philosophy of Science, What Is Science?*, and two books co-authored with Gopal Guru – *The Cracked Mirror: An Indian Debate on Experience and Theory* and more recently, *Experience, Caste and the Everyday Social*. His book titled *JRD Tata and the Ethics of Philanthropy* was published in 2020. He is the Co-Chief Editor of the Springer *Handbook of Logical Thought in India*, the Series Editor for the Science and Technology Studies Series, Routledge, and editorial advisory member of Leonardo as well as Marg. Sarukkai was a professor of philosophy at the National Institute of Advanced Studies until 2019 and was the Founder-Director of the Manipal Centre for Philosophy and Humanities. He has been actively taking philosophy to different communities and places, conducting philosophy workshops for children and bringing philosophy to the public through his writing in the media and through Barefoot Philosophers. His latest book is *Philosophy for Children: Thinking, Reading and Writing*, and it is being published in English, Hindi, Tamil, Kannada, Malayalam and Bengali.

Albeena Shakil is Professor of English at O.P. Jindal Global University, Sonipat, Haryana. She has authored *Understanding the Novel: A Theoretical Overview*, 2015, and guest edited three issues of *Summerhill: IIAS Review*, IIAS Shimla, and co-edited *JGLR: Women, Law and South Asia*, (Upasana Mahanta and Sameena Dalwai), 2019.

R. Umamaheshwari, an independent writer based out of Shimla, with a PhD in History from JNU, New Delhi, is a former Fellow of the Institut d'études avancées de nantes (Nantes Institute for Advanced Study), and former Fellow, IIAS Shimla. She is author of *From Possession to Freedom: The Journey of Nili-Nilakeci* (2018), *Reading History with the Tamil Jainas: A Study on Identity, Memory and Marginalisation* (2018) and *When Godavari Comes: People's History of a River (Journeys in the Zone of the Dispossessed)* (2014).

Acknowledgements

The present volume is an outcome of a two-day national seminar organized at the Indian Institute of Advanced Study, Shimla, India, on 'Is There an Adequate Theory of Justice?' The seminar was conceived with the active encouragement and support of the then and former Directors of IIAS Shimla, namely, Professors Chetan Singh and Peter Ronald deSouza on the occasion of the two-year-long observation of the Institute's Golden Jubilee. Despite the delayed arrival of this volume, the editors of this volume are indebted and gratified to finally bring this volume to fruition with the hope that it will generate some debate on the themes of justice via injustice.

1   Introduction

Albeena Shakil and Gopal Guru

Arguably justice occupies the central place in the philosophical imagination, political mobilization of the masses and theoretical articulation by the theorists. It continues to inspire thinkers to either provide its radical critique or build on its theoretical premises. Improving upon the original idea of justice, however, is the result of widening disparities among people across different contexts. Justice, indeed, is a source that offers conceptual space for creative reflection and political mobilization. Political mobilization, of course, is aimed at using the concept to one's positional advantage. In India, for example, there are new social assertions that are trying to access justice as a policy alternative rather than an exegetical exercise.

In the Indian context, justice is being discussed more as a policy alternative and less as a serious theoretical challenge. However, the Shimla Institute of Advanced Study decided to foray into the theoretical exploration of the idea of justice. During the two-day interrogative seminar, scholars discussed and reflected upon the following issues: What is an adequate conception of justice? Can there be one? Can we imagine an expansive conception of justice? Did we ever have such a conception of justice in the field of political philosophy, particularly in modern times? What are the conditions for its minimum articulation? And do we have these conditions present in the Indian context? Despite the urge and desire to seek justice, participants frequently veered towards deliberating unredressed or unaddressed injustices instead, hence, the semantic and morphological turn in the title of this volume from justice to injustice.

This volume seeks to move beyond the influential thought experiment undertaken by John Rawls in *A Theory of Justice* (1971). His bedrock of a rational liberal consensus that will resolve the competing claims of freedom and equality in order to offer "justice as fairness" has often been illusory in practice despite its continuing allure and various interpretative and reinterpretative *avatars*. With mounting challenges to both freedoms and equality, Robert Nozick's "entitlement" theory of justice articulated in *Anarchy, State and Utopia* (1974), which was premised upon a minimalist night-watchman state and inalienable individual rights, has frequently tended towards protecting entitled individuals. Michael Walzer's *Spheres of*

DOI: 10.4324/9780429355974-1

Justice: A Defense of Pluralism and Equality (1983) conceived a meaning of equality in the negative experiences of subordination and domination, proposing a "complex equality" through pluralistic distribution of social goods and the primacy of communitarian commitments instead of individual rights, albeit while inadequately exploring those negative experiences.

The chapters in this volume take a measure of these and other influential theories of justice and are demarcated by their crucial articulations of injustice in order to access theories of justice. The chapters are organized into five sets of interrogations and engagements. The first set includes two chapters that engage with the theoretical inadequacies of the Rawlsian theory of justice. The second set of two chapters revisit the evolution of modern conceptualizations of justice in Marx, Ambedkar and Gandhi. The third set of two chapters interrogate transcendental and universalist assumptions of contemporary theories of justice vis-à-vis notions of exceptions and deviations that may in fact often be the norm in postcolonial realities. The volume then moves from the theoretical preoccupation of justice to a chapter about the institutional life of justice and its praxis. And the last chapter engages with concrete instances of movements against injustice to argue for and against the reconcilability of universal and particular paradoxes of justice.

In his chapter, Gopal Guru makes a case for theorizing injustice not as an implicit or assumed part of any theory of justice but as its essential, prerequisite or starting condition or axis. The negative lived experience of humiliation, discrimination and oppression, or the non-ideal theory of injustice, he argues, is crucial for the articulation and constitution of any ideal theory of justice. Terming justice and injustice as Purva- and Uttar-paksha, Guru suggests that despite the two acting as reference points for each other, injustice is in fact independent of theories of justice. Sundar Sarukkai questions universalist presumptions of "rationality" for making ethical judgments by Rawls, Sen and Habermas. He explores alternative structures of rationality offered by the Nyāya, Buddhist, Advaita and Jaina logical traditions, which are arguably more grounded in experiences of injustice, thereby making them more suitable systems of ethical rationality for accessing justice in India.

Sobhanlal Datta Gupta suggests that despite intense contestations, Marx's classical and normative writings were in fact dialectically connected, evolving from a negative to a positive conception of justice, from non-normativity to an alternative normativity based on the unfettered exercise of free labor, with revolutionary praxis acting as the catalyst to complete the spectral vision of justice under communism. Samir Banerjee examines the Gandhian concepts of Swadeshi, Swaraj, Sarvodaya, Ahimsa, Satyagrah and trusteeship to understand justice as both a longing and a necessity. While additionally evaluating post-Gandhian thinking and practice, Banerjee contends that the contingency of substantive justice, which in any case is anthropocentric, may make the act of *tyāg* – giving up something to acquire something – crucial to acquiring justice, especially in times of globalization.

While agreeing with Amartya Sen's rejection of transcendental institutionalism, Partha Chatterjee extends and modifies Sen's idea of comparative justice with a global perspective, to propose a comparative and historical approach towards justice in postcolonial societies where questions of collective justice challenge social choice theories premised on individual choice. He draws a link between the historical legacies of oppression in postcolonial societies and their varied quests for justice through electoral democracy, enlightened despotism, populism, social justice, procedural fairness and substantively just outcomes. Gurpreet Mahajan critiques the lack of emphasis on policy and practice in universalist theories of justice. By examining policy debates in the event of the 2013 Uttarakhand flash floods and landslides, she contends that fraudulent practices by technocrats have the potential to undermine and impair the very principles of justice that ostensibly inform them. She suggests that while all theories of justice assume some states of exception, in everyday life exceptions are usually the norm; therefore, questions of everyday life need to be integral to the assessment, reformulation and reconfiguration of theories of justice.

Sanjeeb Mukherjee traces the evolution of a shift away from a combination of self-preservation or life, liberty and equality in Hobbes and Locke to only liberty and equality in Rawls, Nozick and Amartya Sen. Given that nearly half of the global population now lives in conditions of acute poverty, malnutrition, disease and premature death, he emphasizes the need for a principle of justice centered on the right of every individual to live a full and free life.

R. Umamaheshwari evaluates the narratives of displacement on Native Americans, Dogria Konds of Niyamgiri and the villagers displaced by the Polavaram project on the Godavari river to argue that short-term verticality of justice needs replacement by an expansive horizontal conception that will allow for a space for dissent and even breaking away when the state deviates from its expressed goals of protecting its citizen subjects while still expecting permanent allegiance.

These chapters in the volume offer varied and even contending perspectives and engagements with the many theories of justice; however, we hope that the readers will benefit from the theoretical and experiential emphasis on injustice to evaluate conceptions of justice.

2 Inception of injustice is in the conception of justice

Gopal Guru

Let us begin this chapter with a much-discussed and over-emphasised truth that the socio-political conditions do produce different but enduring asymmetries in society and communities. Such asymmetries in turn push the mainstream idea of justice (Rawls, 1971) into an irresolvable paradox. On the one hand, such an idea remains globally relevant in as much as it creates particularly among the marginalised people hopes, aspirations and motivations leading to the realisation of a better future. Although, the modalities of accomplishment of such a future differ ranging from undertaking conflict to secure justice but also to compete for the realisation of such an idea. But what is central to both the systemic struggle for justice and competition from within the community to get justice is the idea of patience to wait for one's turn rather than through the system that underlies and renews the experience of injustice.

Liberal framework of the realisation of justice, arguably, is more incremental and rectificatory rather than structurally transformative. What is central to the idea of justice is the disposition of being patient and hopeful. Both these human attitudes are driven by the force of reason. Put differently, the idea of reason is embedded in the disposition of being patient. However, remaining patient should not be seen as permanent guarantee that is promised within the liberal framework. In fact, the structural limits of a liberal system create a condition for people to be impatient.[1] But generally speaking, the idea of justice tends to instil in people an enduring sense of patience and as a result they would wait for their turn for an opportunity. It suggests that in the system there is enough for those who are competent and qualified to acquire the positional good. This promise is based on the assumption that the system offers everyone equal opportunity for achieving some degree of progress. On the brighter side, the idea of justice, thus, has been envisioned as an opportunity sphere that not only guarantees people positional good leading to the semblance of egalitarian social order, but it also helps create a decent society by protecting their dignity and self-respect. Thus, it could be argued that the idea of justice does contain a moral horizon that promises both material and moral good. Justice as moral universal can be redeemed in the emergence of a decent society. It is needless to mention that the idea

DOI: 10.4324/9780429355974-2

of justice as a moral horizon does have bearing on the liberal perspective. Arguably, such a horizon is constitutive of the commitment to minimising the widening gap between equality and inequality.

However, conversely, normal understanding which places the idea of justice within the moral horizon stands to be scrutinised within the same horizon. Moral horizon essentially puts every grand idea such as justice to serious scrutiny. It subjects the idea to critical evaluation. Put differently, moral horizon as an evaluative frame offers a ground on which the paradoxical nature of justice becomes intelligible. Thus, the mainstream idea continues to remain elusive. But in the liberal registrar, the acknowledgement of the fact that the world of justice is an elusive idea gets reflected in the theoretical improvement made by scholars of international following.

From the liberal perspective, one may take into consideration theoretical efforts made by some of the critical thinkers whose perceptive research work sought to evaluate the performance of the idea of justice taking the moral horizon as a reference point. Put differently, the efficacy of the idea of justice is evaluated by these thinkers (Dworkin, 2002, Cohen, 2008, Shelby, 2007) against the perceived version of moral horizon. In fact, in the recurring context of ever-growing social asymmetries, justice as moral horizon makes its own evaluation not only a possibility but a moral necessity. It is a necessity because it offers reasonably a critical account of such asymmetries that are the result of human interests which are both competitive and in perpetual conflict.

It is needless to mention that justice when evaluated against its own claim of universal moral good (Rawls, 1971), however, tends to expose its own limits. Put differently, justice when it is on its way to the realisation of proclaimed universal claims exposes its own limits. Such limits are evident in the ever-increasing demand for affirmative actions by different marginalised social groups. Limits that are inherent in justice as seed idea, in effect, keep motivating, from time to time, some of the socially sensitive thinkers (Dworkin, 2002, Cohen 2008, Shelby, 2007) who then make sustained theoretical efforts to not only point out such inadequacies, but seeks to minimise such inadequacies by building on to the very idea of justice. In this regard, it is important to keep in view that such scholarly efforts do not seem to produce parallel theories that would then compete with the main idea of justice even for achieving epistemic equivalence. Arguably, such theories, indeed, are supportive of rather than superior to mainstream ideas of justice. They are more rectificatory than the replacement of the main theory.

As mentioned above, in such theoretical attempts, justice as moral horizon has provided the main reference point in the context of which the emergence of supportive theories of justice could be understood. The larger discursive argument can also be made that it is these 'extended theories' that make the seed concepts theoretically intelligible. It needs to be duly acknowledged that such theories, which fall in the same liberal framework, do help appreciate the enduring relevance of efficacy of the mainstream idea of justice.

Put differently, these supportive theories of justice tend to perfect justice as seed idea. They rather revitalise the original mainstream idea rather than repudiate it. These additional theories of justice seek to expand the core meaning of the mainstream idea of justice by throwing light on inadequacy that is inherent in the latter. However, such theories that are built upon the seed idea of justice do not help us understand what is invisible in the very seed concept of justice. Injustice as a social reality is assumed rather than theoretically analysed or morally assessed. They do not inform us about the fact that the inception of injustice lies in the very conception of justice.

The problem of invisibility of injustice which necessarily exposes theoretical inadequacy of the mainstream idea has been pointed out by some of the prominent philosophers who belong to the critical tradition that is aimed at interrogating the thinking that is claimed as classical with timeless relevance. Adorno and Shklar perhaps are excellent examples, who belong to such a critical tradition. Adorno's critique of mainstream theories is evident in his following observation. He says, and I quote,

> A price has to be paid by a subjectively oriented analysis such as epistemology. The price is that ultimately all the concepts it creates prove to be inadequate. Each concept may be said to be an IOU that can be redeemed only by further concept such as Justice, equality and dignity. Expressed more vulgarly, epistemology resembles the man who can only block up one hole by digging another.
>
> (Adorno, 1995: 218-R219)

An insight into the limits of normal theory of justice can be gained from the seminal work done by Judith Shklar. Shklar in her seminal work, *The Faces of Injustice* (Shklar, 1990), has perceptively and sensitively observed that justice is one of the most common subjects in the field of political philosophy since the Greeks. However, she further observes that injustice is a frequent theme in literature (Shklar, 1990) of life but has not been handled by philosophers (Shklar, 1990: 15). As many commentators of Shklar have pointed out that she seeks to understand injustice not as an exact opposite of justice (yack, 1991: 1345).

Following Adorno and Shklar, we in this chapter would like to argue that injustice is a concept that has become invisible in the grand concept of justice. The current chapter, following Adorno, argues that the concept of justice may claim to have provided the most adequate explanation to understand and solve the problem of injustice, and yet, such claims to adequacy are complete only in the absence of the theoretical understanding of injustice.

The affirmative thrust of the language of justice does acquire universal fluency in terms of its 'ought' dimension.

Thus, the grand idea of justice acquires fluency in affirmative language only at the abstract, hypothetical level. In fact, such an idea draws its validity from the hypothetical construction of moral universe. Arguably, the idea of justice, in order to become part of universal system of thought and enjoy universal epistemic status along with other ideas such as liberty and equality, does not have to depend on empirical reality such as injustice. In this regard, it could be argued that the affirmative idea of justice does require a deontological ground in order to travel around the globe. Hence, the concept of injustice is an inseparable axis of justice. But injustice in discursive sense remains a flat ground lacking explanation in the grand theory of injustice.

In the general and perhaps 'normalised' understanding of justice, theoretical claims have often been made to treat affirmative ideas of justice as an epistemologically adequate ground for steering society in an egalitarian direction. It is true that in such understanding injustice as social reality exists only at the level of assumption and not at the level of adequate theoretical reflection. We will further argue that the tautological thrust of the theory of justice involving affirmative language essentially flows from the top to bottom. This flow and the affirmative tone of the language through which such a flow is regulated is built up around the 'ought' question. Justice would suggest what ought to be the life of a person or a group of people. Affirmative language acquires fluency in articulating the 'ought' question or the question of hope and aspirations that decides the linear direction to live the life with fairness. However, affirmative articulation of the idea of justice, howsoever fluent it may be, by its very logic, may not take into reflective consideration the obverse side of justice. The obverse side arguably is injustice. Injustice as negative morality is constitutive of experience of the marginalised and discriminated. Following Shklar, we will argue that negative morality of injustice plays formidable role in critically appreciating and ultimately redeeming the canonised or universally fluent concepts of justice.

However, it perhaps fails to take us to the very depth of the experience of injustice. At the epistemological level, the concept of justice may achieve new heights in terms of normative understanding, but at the ontological level it, however, may not help us reach the depth in understanding the myriad forms of injustice. Put differently, the idea of justice does offer epistemological space to take flight, while the idea of injustice ontology connects us to undergrounds that underlie and renew everyday forms of grotesque social reality. Interestingly, injustice is the underground of the very epistemic ground on which the theory of justice stands. Hence, it would be unfair to separate the principle of justice from injustice.

This raises the valid question, is there a reasonable ground on which the claim to theorising injustice can be sustained? One could offer the following possible grounds on which the claim to theorising injustice could be defended.

First, the lived experience and the practice of injustice as undertaken by the tormentor provide the possibility of making an elevated sense of injustice as social reality. It also offers the much-needed account of the negative terminology which lacks its elaboration in the modular theory of justice. Put differently, its justification as an independent theoretical enterprise lies in its promise to enrich our understanding of complex social reality of which it is an integral part. Second, the chapter also promises to explore the nature of vocabulary that would help us establish both analytical rigour of the concept of injustice and would provide to those who may be interested in taking this line of inquiry forward. The chapter would make an attempt to account for the semantic movement of vocabulary from its empirical expression to its theoretical articulation. The chapter further argues that it is the political force of the movements that takes this vocabulary to higher levels of abstraction and transforms itself from negative into positive or affirmative language. For example, the untouchables' political mobilization led by Bhimrao Ambedkar involves such an affirmative transformation thus converting the Bahsihkrut or ghettoised or ostracised untouchables or popularly called untouchables of India (India with her comprehensively excluded untouchables) into a Puraskrut or Buddhist or inclusive India. The purpose of the chapter is to work out the relationship between the theory of injustice and justice or the non-ideal and ideal theory respectively. Theory of injustice can be understood as non-ideal as it deals with negative experience that is the part of unhappy conditions whereas Rawlsian theory succeeds only in happy circumstances.

We would argue that the emergence of various kinds of movement with emancipatory thrust may have justice at an ultimate end to achieve, but these historical efforts for emancipation necessarily emerged against an immediate context of injustice. However, at the discursive level, what has been however theorised is the ultimate and not the immediate or justice and not injustice.

First, injustice takes shape in the normative limits of the social. These limits are visible in the socially and civilisationally recalcitrant attitude associated with the social practices of touchable castes and perpetuated by casteism in the Indian case and racism in case of the US. Injustice which is constitutive of such recalcitrant social systems refuses to acknowledge the lived experience of discriminated social groups such as dalits in India and the blacks in the US. Such a social system puts these groups from the margin at the receiving end of contemptuous and morally disciplinary gaze of the white racist in the US and upper caste in India respectively. In such a society, a living human being is rendered invisible on the ground that blacks and dalit cannot appear in the public without the sense of anxiety of being tracked down for the malignant purpose of discrimination and humiliation. One could, therefore, argue that in the semantic grammar, the lower case of injustice is deprivation, discrimination and humiliation, and the higher case of justice is equality, mutual respect and dignity.

Second, injustice as lived experience is in front of the victim or confronting the latter. In fact, confrontation with the experience of injustice occurs particularly in the local configuration of power that articulates through

Brahmanism and capitalism. There is an ontological link between the experience of injustice and local configuration of power. It is this either rhetorical support or complete rejection of caste issues by the upper castes that forced the non-Brahmin and dalit thinkers to focus on the question of injustice rather than justice. During the 19th-century and early 20th-century India, the nationalist focus was mainly on justice from the colonial configuration of power. However, such a skewed focus led the non-Brahmin and dalit thinkers to think that justice would not create any impact on the recalcitrant nationalist who had the skewed notion of political freedom as justice rather than treating society as the sphere of injustice. Arguably the imperial state in India, with some sense of liberalism, did pay some sympathetic attention to social question of caste being one of the core questions. Hence it is for these twin reasons the dalit and Bahujan (majority of the marginalised) thinkers notably Jotirao Phule and Babasaheb Ambedkar sought to put injustice before justice and chose relevant conceptual vocabulary, such as muka, the silenced (Ambedkar, 1920), or Bahishkrut (socially ostracised) or the broken men (Ambedkar),[2] which not only sought to interrogate the language of the social elite, but it also helped Ambedkar in the socio-political mobilisation of the dalit masses. In this regard, it is interesting to note that the thinkers from the Bahujan tradition starting from Buddha 4th century BC down to Jotirao Phule in 19th century and Ambedkar in early 20th century, have used the negative language such as Duhkha (suffering)'Gulamgiri" or slavery in Jotirao Phule and Bahishkrut in Ambedkar (Slavery, 1873, Ambedkar, 1928). These thinkers invoked the negative language only an initial semantic condition to articulate the problem of injustice.

In such a vicious form of society which is constitutive of caste system in India and racism in the US, the recalcitrant attitude among the socially dominant sections continues to persist and remains active in destroying the moral foundation of society. It is needless to mention that such foundation is constitutive of normative value such as compassion; compassion that is necessary for educating our moral consciousness about the bad implication of injustice. Ethics has a rich property of reflection, self-examination that helps one to turn towards the other with compassion and friendship and love. Ethics play an important role in making the tormenter aware about his/her own ethical limits. In fact, ethical limits tend to define the recalcitrant propensity within the tormentor who refuses to refrain from doing injustice to other.[3] Recalcitrant attitude, on the contrary, thrives on the regressive reason that is at the service of the need to remain socially and racially dominant. In such social context, the regressive nature of reason provides the ground both for the persistence of injustice and resistance against it.[4]

In this regard, we need to keep in mind, the lived experience of injustice that does provide fertile grounds for theorising grotesque social (reality). The nature of the language is qualifiedly different from the affirmative vocabulary through which the idea of justice is processed. The language of injustice is negative in the sense that it is ontologically linked to experience which lacks positivity. The experience of injustice is constitutive of exploitation, discrimination, deprivation and humiliation. The resultant language of the experience of injustice conceptually approximates itself into the idea, for example of broken men, Bahishkrut, untouchables and the Muk. All these categories which are part of Ambedkar's thinking and dalit mobilisation through social and political movement[5] can provide an epistemic basis for the possible theory of injustice. The immediate empirical language such as Bahishkrut (ostracised) which operates in the everyday forms of social relations on every day basis does emanate from negative experience of the untouchables but is irreducible to such negativity. This is because in unilinear mode it transcends itself to become Puraskrut connoting the sense of fairness, or the just and decent treatment.

However, the social experience of caste, for example, does not provide an automatic advantage for dalit to embark on the theory of injustice. Such experience provides only the objective condition that on their own may not ignite within the victim the subjective will and epistemic capacity to theoretically reflect on such conditions. Put yet differently, injustice as a theoretical problem does exist in the very conception of justice. Such theorisation of injustice, in fact, is the result of inadequacies that are inherent in the grand theory of justice. In fact, it is already and always silently present in the very conception of justice. For example, in the context of the nationalist imagination of India the very conception of the political justice underlined the very existence of injustice emanating from the caste question. The political justice was so paramount on the heads of the nationalist, that they opposed[6] the very idea of justice that was being articulated by some of the liberal-minded nationalist. The aim of the social conference was to address the caste question rather than completely eradicate it as a structural problem.

Similarly, it is also possible to make an elevated sense of the experience of humiliation. Experience of humiliation does not possess a barebone character. Moreover, a person who is at the receiving end of such an experience does not endlessly endure it. In fact, it does its recipient to develop self-reflection and political resistance against the former. Humiliation which empirically occurs to a person essentially gets defined in terms of an active claim that is based on sound reason. Put more clearly, a person who claims to have been humiliated has to have reason in order to defend such a claim. Further to it such a claim to humiliation has to be based on grounds that are universally valid and hence are publicly defendable. For example, the act of refusing to take notice of the physical existence of a person in visual sense or to arbitrarily restrict the physical movement of a person in automotive sense or withdrawing from touching a person in tactile sense and to refraining from using the power of speech in communicating with others, all these acts provide sound grounds on which the claim to humiliation can be defended. Treating some people as untouchable or reducing them to the subhuman level of 'walking carcass', or a 'moral menace' or a 'moving dirt' provides every reason to the person to feel humiliated. It is unfair to deprive a person of the civilisational resources such as seeing, touching and speaking.[7] Thus civilisational violence, in moral sense, offers a sound reason for such people to make a claim that one is humiliated. Thus, it could be theoretically argued that humiliation is a claim which is based on sound reason. Of course, giving reason falls within the liberal framework just as justice as a grand also falls within the same framework but with affirmative thrust.

In this common theoretical context, it is necessary to remind ourselves of the methodological difficulty which makes it annoyingly problematic to completely disentangle injustice from justice. Put differently, it has to be acknowledged that without the epistemic grip of justice, it indeed is difficult to put full theoretical confidence and rigour in the concept of injustice. Put differently, it is the domain of justice rather than injustice that is the source of forward-looking reason, while injustice, as some may argue, is based on reason that may appear to be cynical, shrill and grotesque or beyond the forward-looking reason. It is in the realm of injustice that the seeds of justice reside. It is the experience of injustice which performs an important epistemic function in as much as it seeks to theoretically graduate reasons to the much more mature, robust theoretical articulation of justice. In fact, giving reason or account of injustice is the part of liberal theory. Justification comes from justice. Thus, force of reason that is deployed to sustain the claim for humiliations have its origin in justice and its articulation in injustice.

Similarly, assertion against discrimination which is constitutive of injustice is a sort of moral claim which has to be defended by providing sound reason that eventually belong to the realm of justice. It could be argued that discrimination as an experience cannot be abstracted at the higher levels of its intelligibility without taking into consideration the associated concept of an 'active self' who is motivated by the power of sound reason to be treated equally with others. Injustice is not something that is wrong in the predisposition of a servile person. A person who is at the receiving end of the experience of injustice feels prompted to assert either through writings or protest/movements about his/her experience of discrimination only in the structural conditions. For example, the development of the sense of active individual self among the colonised body of people takes shape in the dual configuration of power: the colonial[8] and the local.[9] Colonised dalit generates the critical consciousness in critical response to the colonial state and active resistance to the local configuration. It is in the local configuration dalit sense of injustice is more acute. It is the liberal sense of being human as compared to the upper castes that makes the case against injustice immanent. The social aspiration to share equal human worth is the reasonably taken step that seeks transcendence from injustice. Conversely, socially produced disability such as untouchability that effectively lead to an inability to occupy the same public space and common cultural resources without giving any publicly defendable ground necessarily leads to discrimination.[10] It is in this fundamental sense discrimination does constitutive injustice.

The experience of discrimination ingrained with injustice becomes intelligible only through the theoretical and political intervention of active agency. Speaking openly against an experience that does not occur is not done with the act of arbitrary will. In fact, formation of such a will is necessarily mediated by the structural dynamics. One could understand the crucial role that such dynamics seem to have played in dalit struggle against injustice.

The early arrival of certain discriminated castes to potent articulation against different forms of discrimination has to be attributed to the structural logic.[11] This logic involved the 19th-century migration of certain untouchable castes from rural to urban India. This migration was quite prominent in the western part of the country, particularly from Maharashtra. For example, the Mahars, the untouchable castes from Maharashtra, due to the lack of dignified employment in the villages had to migrate to different cities in the state of Maharashtra. The modernising process such as education, industrialisation and communication did prompt these lower castes to take some advantage of the fruits that accrued from such processes. It is also evident that such processes underlie and renew the element of unfairness. For example, the Mahars were denied entry into certain well-paid sections of the textile mills in Mumbai, although they were most qualified to join these sections (Ambedkar, 1989: 68).

Thus, it could be argued that the development of critical consciousness against the experience of unfairness is neither natural nor innately present within the agency. In fact, it is the result of the changes in the structures and inauguration of several modernising processes. However, objective condition forms a necessary formative context for the assertion against discrimination. However, for a full theoretical understanding of discrimination, it becomes necessary to understand the emergence of an agency among the discriminated groups. Active agency emerges through the transcendence of a person from his/her servile consciousness to a higher state of subversive, revolting being. Arguably, since a servile person's moral consciousness does involve a normalised content of injustice, it is this form of consciousness that has to be theoretically as well as practically politically addressed on priority. Ambedkar, in fact, undertakes the priority question seriously and seeks to address this question in his discourse on (in)justice. To demobilise particularly dalit from an internalised sense of injustice is the core concern of Ambedkar's metaphysics of emancipation. His theoretical as well as practical political attempt was to tell the untouchable what they are and where they are, and where they want to go. It is not natural for the untouchables to develop a sense of justice out of nowhere, but it is necessary for them to acquire the cognitive capacity to develop an active political consciousness against injustice and social consciousness for just social order.

Humiliation, discrimination and oppression, all the three social structural phenomena, are the struggle concepts in as much as they are formulated in the act of resistance by the subalterns. This resistance is active both against the self and the other. It prompts the self to resist his/her reification into an experience of injustice as well as it encourages the embattled self to civilise the other who is likely to remain persistently recalcitrant. Arguably, such recalcitrant others are represented by the touchable in India and the white racist in the US. It is in this context one could possibly argue that the theory of injustice may not lead to complacency or its reification thus ultimately turns the emancipatory project anti-utopian. However, in this context, it is important to appreciate the point, theoretical turn towards injustice is not an arbitrary choice made by those who are caught up in historical questions such as caste and gender. It is not a voluntaristic move made by an agency to confront the experience of injustice. Discursive energy and moral awareness of injustice that are arguably required for both theorisation and political articulation ultimately become a possibility on two important counts.

First, it seeks to protest against its unceremonious subsumption under the 'ideal theory of Justice'. Second, it offers much-needed account of the negative terminology which lacks elaboration in the modular theory of justice. Put differently, its essence lies in its capacity to resist the recalcitrant tendency that is inherent in the given theory of justice. However, the chapter argues that the political force of the movements takes this vocabulary to higher levels and transforms itself from negative into positive or affirmative language. Thus, converting the Bahsihkrut or ghettoised India into a Puraskrut or Buddhist or inclusive India forms an integral part of this transformative process.

Some thoughts in conclusion

The purpose of the chapter has been to work out the agnostic relationship between the theory of injustice and justice or the non-ideal and ideal theory respectively. Theory of injustice, if at all it is a possibility, can be understood as a non-ideal theory as it deals with negative experiences that are part of unhappy conditions. Conversely, Rawlsian theory succeeds only in happy circumstances. The chapter has argued that injustice is an external shell whereas justice is its inner core which is affirmative and universal in its scope as well. What one, therefore, needs to understand is the following: if one is interested in breaking open from one's shell (injustice) and becoming part of the affirmative/universal core value such as justice, then one has to implicate into one's critical gaze, those universal structures or the material conditions that push social groups into such a shell. Breaking out of the shell results from the mediation of the particular with the universal. To put that differently, one particular cannot mediate with another. For example, Madigas, one of the untouchable castes of Andhra, cannot become part of the universal through confronting the Malas another untouchable caste from the same region. One particular[12] which is locked up with another in the conflict around the issue of reservation, however, seeks to become another particular instead of becoming the universal. It is the subjective consciousness sustained by objective/structural conditions that offers ground for both theoretical and political articulation of the experience of injustice. This is not denying that subjective expression of injustice becomes emotionally quite powerful in as much as it has a redemptive impact on the recalcitrant other.[13] It is also true that such emotional response to the experience of injustice has rectificatory impact on the recalcitrant other. However, ethical roles that belie emotions in generating redemptive impact has its limits as it produces exception, for example, Gandhi, and does not become part of moral law wherever one is legislating by oneself and for oneself such law that would prevent him or her from causing injustice to others. However, the emancipatory project of Indian dalit, American blacks or any other marginalised group injustice is an initial and justice as an essential condition.

Notes

1 There are several social groups in India, which arguably appear to be impatient in demanding quota reservation in job and education. These are from lower castes and from the middle or peasant castes.
2 Babasaheb Ambedkar, Vol.1, WSBA.
3 Ambedkar's critique of caste-minded Hindus falls into the category of those who are considered as recalcitrant.
4 The dalit movement in India and the black movement in the US are two prominent examples.
5 Ambedkar.
6 The so-called nationalist leaders actively and violently oppose an independent assertion of some of the liberal nationalist who tried to bring in focus he question of social injustice. Some the conservative nationalist from Congress party did oppose the social reform efforts made by social conference started by some liberal Congress leaders.
7 The untouchables in India and the blacks in America were violently deprived of such civilisational resources.
8 Comprising the British colonial power.
9 Comprising the capitalism and Brahmanism.
10 Chavdar tank movement for drinking water in 1927 and temple entry movement in 1930s, at Mahad, in Ratnagiri and Nashik District of Maharashtra.
11 The Mahars of Maharashtra and the Malas of Andhra Pradesh or the Jatvas or the chamars of Uttar Pradesh arguably have arrived at such articulation against the discrimination relatively earlier to other dalit castes.
12 Valmikis against Chamar in Uttar Pradesh, Mahars against Matanga in Maharashtra, Adi Karnataka vs Adi Dravida's in Karnataka, Parays vs Chakliyars in Tamil Nadu, Dom vs Pannas in Odisha.
13 Bhalchandra Phadke's response to Sharan Kumar's autobiography, *Akkar Mashi*.

References

Adorno, Theodor, *Kant's Critique of Pure Reason*, Stanford University Press, Stanford, California

Ambedkar BR, Mukanayak, Fortnightly (Marathi), Mumbai, 1920. *Reprinted in Source Material of Babasaheb Ambedkar, Education Department*, Government of Maharashtra, Mumbai, 1979

Ambedkar, Bhashikrut Bharat, Fortnightly Marathi, Mumbai, 1928. *Reprinted in Source Material of Babasaheb Ambedkar*, Education Department, Government of Maharashtra, Mumbai, 1979

Ambedkar, *Writings and Speeches, Education Department*, Government of Maharashtra, Mumbai, 1989.

Akerman, Bruce, *Social Justice in Liberal State*, Yell University Press, New Haven, 1980.

Cohen, Gerald Allan, *Rescuing Justice and Equality*, Harvard University Press, Cambridge, MA, 2008.

Dworkin, Ronald, *Sovereign Virtue Revisited, Ethics*, Vol. 113, No. 1, University of Chicago Press, Chicago, 2002.

Phule, Jotirao, Slavery, First Published in 1879, Reprinted in the Collected Work (Marathi) Yeshwant Dinkar Phadke ed. *Literary and Cultural Committee*, Government of Maharashtra, Mumbai, 1991. *Collected Work, Malshe.*

Rawls John, *Theory of Justice*, Oxford University Press, New York, 1971

Shelby, Tommie, Justice, Deviance and Drak Ghetto, *Philosophy and Public Affairs*, 2007. pp. 126-160.

Shklar, Judith, *The Faces of Injustice*, Yell University Press, New Haven, 1990.

Yack, Bernard, Injustice and Victim's Voice, *Michigan Law Review*, Vol. 89, No. 6, 1991. pp. 1334–1349

3 Rationality and justice

Sundar Sarukkai

Even though ethics as a discipline has placed enormous value on the theoretical approach to moral terms, it is nevertheless the case that morality is first accessible to us as feelings. The feelings of hurt, betrayal, pleasure and so on are the foundational experiences based upon which they can be further conceptualized. Among these feelings, the feeling of injustice is a powerful one and is the dominant catalyst for conceptualizing ideas of justice. In fact, one might even argue that rarely do we experience anything called 'justice', but we are able to 'understand' it. The shift from the experience of injustice to the understanding of justice is accomplished in different ways: through stories and narratives, through music and through 'rational' principles. The Jātaka tales, for example, are an elaboration of the concept of justice through stories, and in so doing they are attempting to hold on to the spirit of experience in the conceptualization of justice. The move from this experience to a theoretical formulation is one that necessarily invokes basic logical principles such as noncontradiction, implication and so on. If logic is essential to the formulation of ethics, then we can ask whether different kinds of logic will lead to different ethics. Indian logic gives us a different way of looking at the structure of logical rationality. I will argue here that a theory of morality based on Nyāya, Buddhist and Jaina logics offers a more useful and effective approach to the question of justice since it is far more grounded in the experience of injustice.

The concept of justice has many different facets and has always eluded attempts to find a unified conceptualization. For example, Vallentyne (2003) suggests that there are competing accounts of justice such as 'libertarian, contractarian, egalitarian, and so on'. He also argues that there is no 'single determinate concept of justice' but identifies five senses of the term: '*moral permissibility* as applied to distributions of benefits and burdens or as applied to social structures', a sense of 'what we morally owe others', 'limits of legitimate coercion', 'giving each his due' and 'fairness'. There are many other explorations of the meaning of justice and of the term 'just', as well as different domains to which they are applied, ranging from the individual to the social. But in this spread of possible meanings of the concept of justice, there is a lurking sense of inherent rational structures that are

DOI: 10.4324/9780429355974-3

necessary for this concept. The very notion of 'just' involving comparison and methods of evaluation of comparison needs not only an operational and instrumental sense of rationality but also the possibility of rational communicative praxis. The common folklore saying that 'Justice should not only be done but should be seen to be done' captures the important element of sociality inherent in the concept of justice and thus demands certain forms of rational action by its very nature. Justice as something to do with morally owing others demands an explanation of why and what we would owe anybody, and such explanations involve ideas of rationality.

The importance of rationality as an integral component of ethical judgement has been stressed, among others, by Rawls, Sen and Habermas. In doing this, however, the theories of rationality which are used are dominantly of a particular philosophical and intellectual tradition. Claims about some universal idea of rationality are in themselves problematical. MacIntyre (1988) in his book *Whose Justice? Which Rationality?* begins by pointing out the diverse and competing theories of justice and wonders whether rationality can help decide which conceptions seem most reasonable. But he also argues that given the debates on the nature of rationality itself, such a possibility remains difficult to achieve. The loss of a rational public discourse which would help adjudicate different conceptions of justice seems to be on the rise given competing notions of justice and rationality. MacIntyre traces this to Enlightenment reason which strove to find unifying principles of reason by keeping out cultural and individual 'peculiarities'. This leads to the inability today to 'unite conviction and rational justification' (ibid., p. 6). An alternative mode of understanding can be recovered from what Enlightenment 'deprived us', and this recovery is

> of the conception of rational enquiry as embodied in a tradition, a conception according to which the standards of rational justification themselves emerge from and part of a history in which they are vindicated by the way in which they transcend the limitations of and provide the remedies for the defects of their predecessors within the history of that same tradition
>
> (ibid., p. 7).

This makes rationality always a 'concept with a history' (ibid., p. 9). Thus, MacIntyre is arguing for a rational basis for the concept of justice, a 'rational inquiry which is inseparable from the intellectual and social tradition in which it is embodied', which implies that we understand theories and doctrines from their historical and contingent contexts. (The conditions for doing this, we will see at the end of this chapter, are of the kind advanced by Jaina thinkers.) One of the conditions for such tradition-based rationality to be possible is that such traditional enquiry is necessarily made through exemplifications, again a view that resonates very closely with the fundamental structure of rationality as defined in Indian philosophical traditions.

Interestingly, he also points out that this account of traditional rationalities needs to be complemented with accounts from other traditions of rational enquiry, including India and China. In a way, this chapter undertakes this task and attempts to show how such forms of inquiry within Indian philosophical systems answer these larger questions on rationality and justice.

If some notion of rationality is essential to the idea of justice, then it is reasonable to ask the following: if different structures of rationality are present in different traditions, then how do these alternate rationalities lead to different notions of justice? To concretely illustrate this possibility, I will look at alternate logical traditions since the logical is seen as being integral to the rational. So if there are different forms of logic and these have different structures of rationality, will they offer an alternate understanding of the concept of justice?

One of the important notions inherent in rationality is that of 'adequacy'. When we ask for an adequate theory of justice, we need to ask what would constitute being adequate. How is an adequate theory of justice different from a theory of justice? Our conceptions of theory as universal in principle allow us to conceive of a theory of justice independent of its match with the experiences of justice and injustice in the world. In this sense, a theory of justice can be formal and its strength or relevance increases with its capacity to describe, explain and perhaps even predict events related to the idea of justice. Perhaps the most sustained engagement with this link between theory and its domain of applicability comes from philosophy of science. Given the surplus of theories which are postulated in science, the obvious challenge is to understand how one can choose one theory over another. A stronger theory is one that has more explanatory capacity and one that matches with the observations. Sidestepping the challenge of the theory-ladeness view of observations, we can note one particular solution to this problem of relating theory and observation, namely, van Fraassen's account of adequacy. Fraassen (1980) invokes adequacy as an alternative to scientific realism, as a way to respond to realism of unobservable entities. But in so doing, he is suggesting an important change to the traditional claim about scientific theories and their relation to realism. The idea of adequacy stands for what has been called 'constructive empiricism' and is primarily the claim that the task of scientific theories is only to fulfil empirical adequacy as against the claim that scientific theories are literally true. Invoking adequacy in the context of justice, I would argue, also shifts us into the domain of anti-realism about justice as a natural element in the world and thus may be more powerful in handling contemporary challenges to this notion.

Among the many different ways of understanding rationality, it is useful to focus on the idea of justification as being central to rationality. What justifies any cognitive state of ours? If I claim that I am seeing a table, it is an irrational claim if the table is not seeable by me. Being irrational, in our common discourse, is not to heed to reason, to take into account evidence and so on. But what is the most urgent reason to be rational? Perhaps the most urgent and pragmatic reason is that some notion of rational discourse is essential for inter-subjective agreement. Rationality creates the possibility of making 'common' sense of our shared experiences and to be able to think and talk about these collective experiences in a meaningfully shared sense.

Modern accounts of rationality often rest on assumptions around justification. For example, Batens (1978, p. 25) notes that rationality is primarily about justification and what he means by justification is primarily the process that leads to justified beliefs. Dallmayr (1988, p. 557) points out to a similar formulation by Habermas who suggests that rationality is fundamentally linked to knowledge but not the content of it and is more a measure of how we acquire and utilize it. Thus it is useful to understand rationality as a way of justifying and as a process of justification. While concepts such as universality and necessity may be integral to some idea of justification, they are nevertheless subservient to these processes of justification which grounds rationality.

Thus, it is not difficult to see why logic and rationality have often been clubbed together. First of all, logic is primarily about processes and relations, and not about content, such as the content of a syllogism, for example. Logic is also a great tool for justification and convincing others. Logic embodies universality and necessity, and it is reasonable to believe that historically these concepts drew their essential meaning from logic and mathematics. Rationality as expressing practices of human behaviour is also closely linked to logic as an analysis of arguments and as necessarily being bound by rules. Hence, it is no wonder that logic has often been expressed as the 'laws of human thought'. The most fundamental logical rules, such as law of noncontradiction, modus ponens etc., also illustrate how rationality is very closely tied in with logic. In the context of ethics, the attempts to discover the relationship between logic and ethics, and in particular its relation to binary logic, have been influential in the development of modern ethical theories.

If justice is to be available as an objective category, then it must also be a rational category. We would hesitate to say that justice is an individual feeling or an individual matter of opinion since to do that is to negate its usefulness as a concept. However, we must note that the experience of justice is primarily through the experience of its negation, that is, the experience of injustice. It would perhaps be correct to say that the concept of justice is abstracted from real everyday experiences related to injustice. As an abstraction, the concept of justice is already taken into the fold of rationality.

As I mentioned earlier, ethics and rationality are two closely related terms. The many approaches to ethics are fundamentally rational in character, meaning that there is a rational attempt to evaluate, describe and understand ethical actions and ethical judgements through basic principles of rationality such as the principles of logic and universality. Interestingly, Matilal (2007, p. 81) suggests that the concept of dharma should be viewed as a 'theory of moral behaviour' and claims that the tradition of dharma 'developed through an attempt at rational criticism of itself', although it is not clear as to what he means by the use of the term 'rational' here.

It is useful to focus on this relation between logic, rationality and ethics for it allows us a useful way to ask the question of what it means to conceptualize an adequate theory of justice for the Indian context. In this chapter, I am interested in asking a very simple question: if rationality, as broadly described above, is integral to a formulation of justice, then can the rationalities of non-western cultures lead to other conceptualizations of justice? In particular, since the logic of the binary or logic as a particular analysis of arguments have been deeply influential ways of understanding logic, can we look at other logical systems to see what kind of rationality and what kind of notions of justice they support, or at least adequately support?

Here is where it is useful to consider the formulations of Indian logic. As is well known by now, there are alternate formulations of logic in the different Indian philosophical traditions such as Nyāya, Buddhist, Vedāntic and Jaina schools. Since my aim is to illustrate how to draw on alternate logical rationalities, I will briefly discuss the relevance of the logical structures of each of these schools and their connection to formulations of justice.

Nyāya and rational explanation

The Nyāya school of philosophy is known for its extensive literature on logic and is often used synonymously to stand for logical traditions in Indian philosophy, even though there are important contributions by the other schools as well. For purposes of my illustration of alternate modes of rationality, I will look at only one small aspect of the Nyāya logical formulation, namely, its five-step syllogistic process, and show how this syllogism is most usefully seen as a kind of rational explanation, one that is essential to moral explanations.

The five-step process of the Nyāya is given as follows; this is for the example of inferring fire on seeing smoke on a hill.

1. Proposition: There is fire on the hill.
2. Reason: For there is smoke.
3. Example: (Wherever there is smoke, there is fire), as in the kitchen.
4. Application: This is such a case (smoke on the hill).
5. Conclusion: Therefore it is so, i.e., there is fire on the hill.

There has been extensive discussion on the need for the five steps, the meaning of the example term, the relation this structure has with Aristotelian syllogism and so on. In my earlier work I looked at another interpretation of this structure and this interpretation was basically influenced by the literature on the nature of scientific explanations.

The basic claim that science has its own modes of explanation proved to be influential in our understanding of science. One of the first articulations of this is through the deductive-nomological model of Hempel and Oppenheimer where they give a structure of explanations in science. This model suggested that explanations in science are unique, and these structures set science apart from explanations in other fields such as myths, astrology and so on.

The structure of the DN model is as follows (Rosenberg 2000, p. 28):

> The explanation must be a valid deductive argument.
> The *explanans* must contain at least one general law actually needed in the deduction.
> The *explanans* must be empirically testable.
> The sentences in the *explanans* must be true.

An important point to note here is that these conditions allow one to predict as well as explain an already observed fact. Thus, this model is symmetrical between prediction and explanation.

It is quite easy to see the striking parallel between the structure of the DN model and that of the nyāya syllogistic one, and it was this that led me to postulate a way of understanding the nyāya syllogism as a species of scientific explanation (Sarukkai 2005). What nyāya explains through this five-step structure is the inference that we have of inferring fire when we see smoke. Moreover, this structure is a way of describing what is called inference-for-others. Thus, it is a communicative praxis of rationally justifying to another why we make the inference that we do. In other words, the nyāya model is an explanatory model for believing that there is fire when I see smoke. We should also note the important point made in the context of scientific explanations that the DN model allows prediction as well as explanation. This character is extremely important in the context of ethics since ethics is fundamentally related to human action, and most of our actions are based on some measure of prediction, especially in ethical action. Thus, I would argue that the nyāya five-step process not only gives us a model for moral explanations but also defines moral rationality as logical explanation to others thus allowing us to see that morality is about rational explanation.

To support this view, we should first understand moral judgements as also being inferential in character. Moral qualities are not directly perceived. To recognize someone is ethically 'good' or a particular act is a 'good' act is only possible as inferential cognition. There is something in the act that suggests its moral status. There are some other pointers which might mitigate against such an inference. Whatever be the case, the possibility of having moral cognitions brings such judgements into the domain of logic, which is nothing but the analysis of inferences. Such a possibility of understanding moral actions supports an experiential reading of morality, and particularly of making sense of the experience of justice. In other words, while experientially it is the feeling of injustice that seems to matter, the feeling of justice is recovered through the experience of an inferential cognition of justice. What I am suggesting here is a way to meaningfully use the vocabulary and tools of Indian philosophical systems for contemporary analysis of the concept of justice.

Buddhist logic and the semiotics of moral actions

In a similar way, we can extend this analysis to Buddhist logic. As far as inferential cognitions are concerned, there is a similarity to a large extent in the conceptual framework of the Indian logical systems. The Buddhist analysis of inference, following Dinnaga's influential framework, is another useful way to interpret and analyse moral concepts such as justice. Dinnaga reduces inference to an analysis of signs and thus brings it under the ambit of semiotics. He formulated the 'triple nature of the sign', three conditions which a sign must fulfil in order that it leads to valid inference (Matilal 1998, p. 6).

1. It should be present in the case (object) under consideration.
2. It should be present in a *similar* case or a homologue.
3. It should not be present in any *dissimilar* case, any heterologue.

So, for example, when we see smoke it stands as a sign for fire (although we must note that this is only one of the possibilities). The sign – smoke – is the reason and evidence for the inference and is called the *hetu*. The sign that catalyzes an inference is not restricted to material signs like smoke but can also be conceptual terms.

I am not aware of the use of this formulation to analyse inferential cognitions related to moral actions, but I want to give a motivation for doing so. Firstly, in this Buddhist formulation we have the foundations of a semiotics of morality whereby moral qualities are inferred as valid inferential cognitions. The sign functions as the ground for moral rationality, and I would argue that in our everyday experience of moral judgements, we often infer this from certain signs. Thus, moral rationality through the framework of Buddhist logic would be to understand what signs are needed to decide if an act is moral. As I mentioned above, our judgement about moral actions is often based on perception of other acts. For example, if we see somebody help an old lady cross a busy street, we might infer that the person is a kind person. Most of our commonly accepted moral actions are primarily signs that stand for moral qualities. Buddhist logic is fundamentally about analyzing the relationship between the signs and what they stand for. When applied to actions that can stand for ethical action, we construct an ethical rationality which is about evaluating these judgements. If we want to literally draw upon the way by which Buddhist and in general Indian logical traditions do this, then we would look for the relation of vyapti between the sign and the signified. For example, we could say that not all acts are valid signs for inference but some acts are and those are what we would call ethical actions.

The difference between a western philosophical approach and the Buddhist approach can be illustrated by this example. Suppose we see a person helping an old lady cross a busy road. This can be seen as an ethical act and the analysis of it will normally begin by analyzing the act of helping. Thus, 'helping to cross the road' in itself becomes the subject of ethical analysis, but for this expression to be amenable to the application of Indian logic, we would need to specifically include the agents who perform this action. Thus, this rationality necessitates that our analysis should always be about 'A helping B to cross the road' instead of merely an analysis of the term 'helping to cross the road'. Incomplete relations cannot be legitimate objects of ethical enquiry – only embodied action is a correct term for ethical analysis. The relational expression is not a proper subject for analysis, and action has to be embodied and exemplified in order to make it ethically meaningful. Such a perspective, common in general to the many Indian philosophical traditions, is an alternate rationality on which questions of ethics are to be founded. Similarly, the statement that 'Killing is wrong' is not a legitimate object of inquiry as compared to 'A killing B is wrong'. Such expressions go against specific notions of universality that characterize dominant western ethical theories, but they are also the potential solutions for the problems that characterize these theories.

Advaita and the question of justice[1]

I want to point out a slightly different form of rationality that is at the heart of certain social practices in the Indian society by drawing on a particular case of the use of advaita by the great social reformer, Narayana Guru, who uses advaita to develop his own emancipatory politics for the oppressed castes. The question of justice in advaita (and in general, within Indian philosophical systems) is important for another reason: many commentators seem to find a lack of engagement with themes of justice and equality in mainstream Indian intellectual traditions. This does not imply that there are no statements which promote the value of equality of humans and indeed the equality between humans and animals. But what they seem to find is the lack of an engaged theoretical discussion on the notions of justice and equality. We should note that this lack of engaged 'theory' is not restricted to these themes but to the larger discipline of ethics itself. Matilal, for example, echoing many others, points to the lack of the development of an independent discipline called ethics in Indian thought. While this does not in any way imply that Indian philosophical traditions did not engage with matters of right and wrong, the way they went about it was not in a 'theoretical mode' – that is, basing their arguments on universal principles, for example.

But how then did they articulate their ideas of a term like equality? Even if it was in terms of stories, how was that theme manifested? I am focusing on the idea of equality for two reasons: one, even in contemporary theories of justice, equality is a central principle, and two, in the context of caste practices, equality becomes an important category. When Narayana Guru calls for one caste for all humans, he too is basing it on the simple observation that all humans belong to one common category and are equal in that sense. In the traditional Indian context, there is, ironically, a larger space of equality in that animals and humans are put into the same category: this implies, among other things, transmigratory moves from the animals to humans and vice versa. Thus, the common principle that binds all these observations and stories is that not all entities are the same but they are all equal, although how exactly they are equal remains a metaphysical enquiry.

So, even if one grants that these philosophical systems were responding to certain themes related to equality, we still have another problem: how then is inequality justified in social practice? In other words, to discover a larger coherent discourse of equality, one can begin with the justifications for inequality, something which is easily found in these philosophies. And in the context of contemporary thought, we would do well to remember that equality has become a dominant notion in any discussion on justice, especially post-Enlightenment. As Sen (2009, p. 291) points out, 'every normative theory of social justice' demands 'equality of *something*'.

I would argue that caste inequality is sustained by a process of naturalization and that this marks out the speciality of caste experience. There have been many attempts to naturalize inequality. The invocation of race, brain size, colour and caste are potent examples of the attempt to justify inequality between individuals and groups by taking recourse to some natural characteristic. The inequality in society faced by women, Blacks, Dalits and others is but a reflection of the success of this naturalizing tendency. As discussed in Guru and Sarukkai (2012), even untouchability gets naturalized and becomes a property of an individual.

One way by which caste gets naturalized is through its association with karma. Weber's argument that karma legitimized the caste system was an influential one. Echoing popular variations on the theme that the present status one has is a consequence of past actions in earlier births, Weber, as Milner (1993) points out, went on to argue that rejecting one's caste belongingness would be punished in future reincarnations. Many writers have rejected Weber's claims on various grounds, and the many complex and local narratives of karma point to the limitation of Weber's view. However, the idea that one pays in the present what one has sowed not just in this life but in earlier ones is a theme that is replayed over and over again from vedāntic texts to folk tales. What is most surprising is that we see this in popular narratives of caste in today's society, particularly from the growing strident voice of upper castes that are against the caste mobilization of the other castes. We also see this very stridently in the narratives of genetics and its relation to caste. In fact, both these arguments (karma and genetics) are a form of naturalization of caste. It is obviously so in the case of genetic determination of caste but in the case of karma, it is a little more complex. Elements of this naturalization may also be present in the capability approach mentioned above.

Milner goes on to develop the relation between caste and eschatology in Hindu thought. The relation between caste and Hindu eschatology, for Milner, is possible because both of them are 'systems of structured inequality' (Milner 1993, p. 302). He goes on to list three central features of caste: one, the lack of mobility across (relatively many) caste boundaries, caste membership based solely on 'inheritance and ascription', and significant energy devoted to maintaining caste distinctions (ibid., p. 303). He then argues that the three major elements of Hinduism, namely, samsara, karma and moksa, are the structural inversions of these three characteristics of caste.

Samsara is mobility across births. As Milner correctly notes, religious texts have continuously stressed how a sinful life will lead to birth in a lower caste, and the key point here is that in Hinduism, there is continuous mobility across births but no mobility in this world (ibid., p. 304). This recognition that this worldly existence is incomplete – at least for final judgements of any kind – is fundamental to how we conceptualize ethics and inequality in Hinduism. This will also lead us to reconsider the question of inequality among castes.

Karma as merit, according to Milner, is the structural reversal corresponding to the second characteristic of caste: that caste is based on inheritance and ascription. As Kane points out (quoted in ibid., p. 305), the law of karma makes existence deterministic. The law of karma is a true law of justice which works across many births instead of just one. It also points out that a principle of justice and of inequality restricted to the world is always *underdetermined* and hence cannot be exhausted by enworlded situations.

So to answer what exactly is unequal in a caste hierarchy, it is necessary to broaden, not the 'space' of equality, which Sen rightly criticizes, but the 'time' of equality. First of all, the very notion of equality has to be broadened to take into account this intergenerational karmic process. Within this process, there are at least two distinct domains of inequality: one is the *local inequality* (inequality in the present world) and the other is a *generational equality* (equality across rebirths). In other words, the domain over which we sum equality or inequality is not just of the experiences of this world but experiences across rebirths. In the overall generational whole, equality is not only sustained but is enshrined as a fundamental principle. But in the localized mode of one existence, equality is not guaranteed. One simple analogy of the different perspectives of the global and the local is a circle: when looked at closely, a segment of the circle is a line. To understand the full nature of the circle we have to reconstruct all these local lines. Something analogous is at the basis of a larger ethical theory based on karma. It is easy to see how themes in justice map out in this theory, such as the relation between retributive justice and generational equality.

The principle of 'generational equality' is that all human beings are completely equal when counted across generations. One is always in a transient caste in this life because you don't know which caste you will belong to in your next life, if you are reborn as a human in the first place! The twice born nature of brahminhood is only an allegory of the repeated birth one takes through rebirths and the possibility that one has to recapture past caste affiliations in each rebirth. The problem of caste inequality at an experiential individual level is negated through this argument that the state of being in a caste is only temporary – even for the untouchables. That is, in the narrative of karma, an untouchable can go out of that state and be reborn in a caste or even attain liberation and not be reborn as a human at all. And equally, a Brahmin who does not practise what he is supposed to can be reborn into any other caste or as an untouchable or even as an animal.

Thus, one might understand this to say that across generations, across the span of rebirths, there is a fundamental principle of equality. This is not the equality of human individuals but the equality of individual souls. In other words, the most fundamental principle of equality is given to the essence of the embodied humans, their souls. Souls have no caste, no class. They do not carry these 'temporal' markings but only 'value' markings. In their very embodiment they lose their equality, and it is these embodied humans who now carry the possibility of inequalities.

Is it possible to consider this fundamental principle of equality of all beings, not in their temporal embodied manifestation but across the span of rebirths, as a principle of justice in any philosophy that upholds the doctrine of karma? This is a difficult question since this only gives a 'rational' account of inequalities through formulating principles of justice that seem to be transcendental. I would argue that this is a classic instance of how the concept of 'equality' differs from that of 'justice'. Even though there could be such rational accounts of inequality among individuals (such as through the doctrine of karma or through the doctrine of merit and work in contemporary public discourse), I would nevertheless not consider them as meaningful theories of justice. The continued experience of injustice which arises in cases of such inequalities points to the danger of rational reconstructions, particularly in the moral domain. The inequality which characterizes caste hierarchy should be seen as inequalities which arise by the very act of embodiment of these souls and thus are representations of an 'embodied inequality'. The metaphysical grounding of these hierarchies arises at the first instance of embodiment and birth. Thus, it should be no surprise that the moment of birth is so fundamental to the dialectic opposition which sustains caste, namely, the hereditary inherence of caste in both the Brahmins and the Untouchables. The injustice in these caste practices cannot be rationally reduced to certain operations across generations but must respond to the lived situations of every individual in their moment of existence.

Jaina logic and the epistemology of morality

Finally, I want to explore the possible relationship between a completely different notion of rationality in the context of the ideas of justice and other moral terms, one developed from the logical tradition of the Jainas. Jaina logic is unique in many ways and its emphasis and articulation of non-binary logic is remarkable for many reasons. I want to suggest here that the rationality associated with Jaina logic can be of great use in constructing ethics based on its rationality.

The three core elements of Jaina logic are those of the doctrine of many sidedness (anekāntavāda), standpoint view (nayavada) and sevenfold predication (syādvada). Cort (2000) points out that anekāntavāda is a 'combination of two logical tools' – nayavada (seven standpoints) and syādvada (sevenfold predication). In principle, there are infinite perspectives but the Jainas use only seven; seven classes or modes contain all possible perspectives. These seven types are a common point of view (about particulars), general point of view (about universals), practical point of view, here-and-now point of view, verbal point of view, subtle (etymological) point of view, and restriction to a single meaning. Each of these views is a partial view. So, a 'judgement is impartial only if it encompasses all seven points of view' (ibid., p. 326).

This metaphysical basis of the Jaina view leads to the well-known sevenfold predication of Jaina logic through the use of the syāt operator. As Koller (2000, p. 404) points out, syāt 'transforms a categorical statement into a conditional statement'. Thus, when we have a statement 'x is y' and the syāt operator acts upon it, the sentence gets modified as follows: syāt (x is y) = 'qualified in the appropriate ways a, b, and c, x is y'. The doctrine of anekāntavāda – 'doctrine of non-onesidedness' – is a very simple phenomenological principle of the many perspectives as constituting reality. Thus, every statement and assertion of reality is only partial and to be truthful it has to explicitly account for the perspective from which it is being articulated. As Priest (2008) argues, this explicit element is the 'syāt'. Sometimes syāt is translated as maybe, perhaps, arguably and so on. But what this contributes is that it adds a new truth value other than the usual true and false. So now the truth values for Jaina logic become true, false and 'non-assertable'. There has been a significant amount of debate on what this 'non-assertable' could mean since this value can be 'both true and false' or 'neither true nor false'.

If we follow the logic of the syāt, then any statement that we make has to explicitly note the standpoint from which it is made. All statements, according to syādvada, can be placed within seven types – as a combination of positive and negative attribution and nature of expressibility (what Priest would call as non-assertable). Cort (2000) describes these seven types as follows:

- From a certain perspective, the table exists.
- From a certain perspective, the table does not exist.

- From a certain perspective the table exists, and from another perspective it does not exist.
- From a certain perspective, the nature of the table is inexpressible.
- From a certain perspective the table exists, and from another perspective the nature of the table is inexpressible.
- From a certain perspective the table does not exist, and from another perspective the nature of the table is inexpressible.
- From a certain perspective the table exists, and from another perspective the table does not exist, and from a third perspective the nature of the table is inexpressible.

This can equivalently be seen as the Jaina theory of sevenfold division (sapt-abhangi) which is that 'a sentence may have one of seven truth values'. Thus, a sentence has seven predicates describing its semantic status. Seen in this way, we can interpret the above seven types as expressing specific kinds of truth values. Priest uses 'arguably' instead of 'from a certain perspective' and describes these seven types of truth values as follows:

- Arguably, it (i.e. some object) exists. The first predicate pertains to an assertion.
- Arguably, it does not exist. The second predicate pertains to a denial.
- Arguably, it exists; arguably, it does not exist. The third predicate pertains to successive assertion and denial.
- Arguably, it is non-assertable. The fourth predicate pertains to a simultaneous assertion and denial.
- Arguably, it does not exist; arguably, it is non-assertable. The fifth predicate pertains to an assertion and a simultaneous assertion and denial.
- Arguably, it exists; arguably, it is non-assertable. The sixth predicate pertains to an assertion and a simultaneous assertion and denial.
- Arguably, it exists; arguably it doesn't exist; arguably it is non-assertable. The seventh predicate pertains to a successive assertion and denial and a simultaneous assertion and denial.

The importance of this formulation must not be underestimated, which we might tend to do because of our immersion in binary values of true and false. What I want to suggest here is that this traditional, rational structure is a powerful tool when extended to moral statements. Suppose I apply this reasoning to a simple moral statement that 'Killing is wrong'. When we apply the Jaina rationality to this assertion, we would have to correctly say 'Under certain conditions, killing is wrong' or 'arguably, killing is wrong'. Explicitly, we would have to say 'under the conditions a, b, c ..., killing is wrong'. It is this statement which is morally correct and helps us avoid major problems in moral assertions. Even in this simple case, we know the difficulty in asserting 'killing is wrong' because there are many conditions under which it is not seen to be morally wrong such as in war, capital punishment, abortion, killing animals and so on. What Jaina rationality contributes to ethical analysis is to explicitly ask for the conditions under which an assertion is made. Just like the verifiability conditions that are seen as constituting meaning of a sentence, so too we can see this argument as providing 'assertability conditions' which is to say that the truth value of an assertion is nothing more than the conditions under which it is assertable.

There is a direct correlation between this form of rationality and moral terms. There has been some discussion on the claim that anekāntavāda is the source of ahimsā, and specifically, what has been called 'intellectual ahimsā'. Part of this argument was based on the observation that the many-sidedness argument of the Jainas led to a tolerant support of their opponent positions also. As Cort notes, it is true that the most faithful representations of other traditions are primarily to be found in Jaina texts, although he disagrees that the Jainas actually practised intellectual ahimsā. But whether anekāntavāda was specifically the 'philosophical expression of ahimsa' is not the point; the rationality associated with this view allows the possibility of an ethical rationality which is not based on problematical claims of universality and necessity derived from the Enlightenment tradition but one that relates traditional rationalities (as described by MacIntyre, for example), embodied actions and our inferential cognition of moral actions. Such an approach is also extremely important in terms of communicative practices related to questions of justice and public debate (Sarukkai 2015).

Note

1 Parts of this section have, in the meanwhile, appeared in my book with Gopal Guru titled *Experience, Caste and the Everyday Social*, Oxford University Press, 2019.

References

Batens, D. "Rationality and Ethical Rationality." *Philosophica* 23, 1978, pp. 23–45.

Cort, J. "'Intellectual Ahimsa' Revisited: Jain Tolerance and Intolerance of Others." *Philosophy East & West* 50, 2000, pp. 324–347.

Dallmayr, F. "Habermas and Rationality." *Political Theory* 16, 1988, pp. 553–579.

Guru, G. and S. Sarukkai. *The Cracked Mirror: An Indian Debate on Experience and Theory*. Oxford University Press, 2012.

Koller, J. M. "Syādvāda as the Epistemological Key to the Jaina Middle Way Metaphysics of Anekāntavāda." *Philosophy East and West* 50, 2000, pp. 400–407.

MacIntyre, A. *Whose Justice? Whose Rationality?* University of Notre Dame Press, 1988.

Matilal, B. K. *The Character of Logic in India*. State University of New York Press, 1998.

Matilal, B. K. "Dharma and Rationality." In *Indian Ethics*, Eds. P. Billimoria et al. Oxford University Press, 2007.

Milner, M. "Hindu Eschatology and the Indian Caste System: An Example of Structural Reversal." *The Journal of Asian Studies* 52, 1993, pp. 298–319.

Priest, G. "Jaina Logic: A Contemporary Perspective." *History and Philosophy of Logic* 29, 2008, pp. 263–278.

Rosenberg, A. *Philosophy of Science.* Routledge, 2000.

Sarukkai, S. *Indian Philosophy and Philosophy of Science.* Motilal Banarsidass, 2005.

Sarukkai, S. "To Question and Not to Question: That is the Answer." In *The Public Intellectual in India*, ed. Romila Thapar et al. Aleph, 2015.

Sen, A. *The Idea of Justice.* Allen Lane, 2009.

Vallentyne, P. "Justice in General: An Introduction." In *Equality and Justice: Justice in General*, ed. P. Vallentyne. Routledge, 2003.

van Fraassen, B. *The Scientific Image.* Oxford University Press, 1980.

4 Marx and justice

Reviewing a contested issue

Sobhanlal Datta Gupta

I

In the 1970s and 1980s, when the influence of Marxism on the academic community was visibly prominent, we witnessed quite an animated discussion on subjects like Marxism and morality, Marxism and justice and other related issues. Significantly, in the repertory of Marxism these have been generally considered as grey areas, the reason being their somewhat marginalized, if not ambiguous, status in Marx's writings. Indeed, Marx's own position on justice and morality was never clearly articulated, resulting in a sharp debate among the interpreters of Marx. One school is of the opinion that Marx considered them simply as relativist concepts, derivatives of class society and thereby reductive notions, which had no intrinsic value. The opponents of this position, however, argue that Marx did harbour an ethical notion of justice, which is implicit in his texts, the suggestion being that this does not square with the relativist position. The understanding is that Marx's vision of a society, free from the exploitation of capital, was essentially grounded in the idea of a moral order based on justice and the very idea of goodness associated with it connects it to ethics.

Consequently, the debate addressed the following questions: (a) Did Marx espouse any moralistic notion of justice, i.e. justice as a normative principle, viewing it in essentialist terms? (b) Did Marx work out a non-essentialist, reductive/derivative concept of justice, considering it as an ideology? This debate was actually reflective of a larger controversy regarding Marx's philosophical anchorage. Those who considered Marx as a theorist of the normative notion of justice refused to accept the argument that this essentialist position necessarily meant resort to idealism, since the relativist understanding implied that it was a defence of materialism per se.

Closely associated with this debate emerged another question: did Marx consider capitalism unjust? The exponents of the first position believe that Marx considered capitalism as a morally unjust order, since he condemned capitalism as an exploitative system, while the advocates of the second position argued that superstructural elements like morality and justice being relative to the production system, for Marx the question whether a

DOI: 10.4324/9780429355974-4

system is just or unjust, moral or immoral, was quite irrelevant. The first position was broadly defended by Norman Geras, Kai Nielsen et al., while the second position was advocated by scholars like Allen W. Wood and Robert Tucker.[1]

II

Another question, a question of a different kind, follows: for Marx, did justice possess a normative value or an instrumental value? Those who locate Marx in a normative framework consider him a humanist, tracing his moral concerns to his early writings, i.e. the *Economic and Philosophical Manuscripts of 1844* (EPM), commonly known as *Paris Manuscripts*, *German Ideology* (1845–46) and such other works. Others who take a relativist and thereby a non-essentialist position view Marx's position on justice as nothing more than instrumentalist in the sense that it is relative to society, economy and the production system. This is an understanding which is normally associated with those interpreters of Marx who consider him a "scientist" and not "humanist", reminding one of the debates initiated by Althusser in the 1970s on the young vs mature or humanist vs scientist Marx.[2]

The purpose of this chapter is not to go back to this old debate, but it cannot be perhaps denied that this debate has an interesting implication for Marx's understanding of justice. On a very sophisticated philosophical level when Althusser critiqued the "humanist" Marx (his famous description of Marxism as "theoretical anti-humanism"), the critique also indirectly vindicated the widely shared understanding of the Communist Parties that justice has only an instrumental value as long as the ideological battle between capitalism and socialism continues, which connotes two meanings for the Marxist praxis. One: for the upkeep of socialism, forced collectivization, surveillance and censorship, regimentation and statism of the highest order are necessary in the name of defence of justice for the majority, i.e. the proletariat, under socialism. The very concept of proletarian dictatorship thus assumed an instrumentalist character. Two: for suppression of counterrevolution and the opponents of socialism penal measures, howsoever inhuman and cruel they may appear, i.e. Gulag, political trials and execution, are nothing wrong, since they are politically correct, serving as instruments for the defence of a just cause, namely, socialism. It is this argument that went into the making of Stalinism, unfolding thereby the infamous legacy of repression, terror and violence, associated with the Soviet and East European models of socialism on the one hand and with the kind of "socialism" that flourished in Kampuchea under Pol Pot or in North Korea under Kim Il Sung and his successors. It is quite evident that the instrumentalist position is essentially political, as distinct from the moral/humanist understanding of justice. This, of course, does in no way suggest that Althusser defended these regimes or endorsed their practices.

But how valid is the contraposition of these two positions, the so-called popular or generally accepted relativist vs normative/essentialist understanding of justice? Perhaps it is necessary and possible to reframe this understanding by breaking the disjunction between these two viewpoints. Two arguments are in order here. First, when Marx takes a so-called non-essentialist and thereby a relativist position on the issue of justice and thereby critiques and dismisses law, rights and justice as nothing more than bourgeois catchwords, he actually points to the necessity of their replacement by a new set of values which would be the constituent elements of the whole man, the new man under communism. This tone is quite evident already as early as 1844 in his *Paris Manuscripts*. The observation of John Rawls in his lectures on Marx is worth noting in this context. Thus, while Rawls broadly agrees with Norman Geras that Marx condemned capitalism as unjust, the question that he raises is quite relevant: did Marx talk of replacement in the name of values like right and justice or in terms of alternative values like freedom, self-realization and humanity.[3] In other words, to cite Rawls, "Finally, the alleged distinction between kinds of values and principles of right and justice vs. values and principles of freedom and self-realization – is shown to be completely arbitrary by Marx's principle of a full communist society".[4] Thus, the apparent paradox in Marx stands resolved. There is a definite shift from his relativist notion of rights, morality and justice, which he considers as nothing but bourgeois sham in texts like *Poverty of Philosophy*, while critiquing Proudhon, or in his *A Contribution to the Critique of Hegel's Philosophy of Right: Introduction* to a normative notion of justice, as evident in *Grundrisse* (1857–58) and *Critique of the Gotha Programme* (1875), which call for the self-realization of man – the transition from a negative to a positive view of justice, from non-normativity to an alternative normativity under communism, which effects a complete rupture with the negative view of justice and morality in the non-communist phase of human history.

It needs to be emphasized at this point that the main reason underlying this debate is rooted in Marx's own ambiguous position on the question of morality. Chinese Marxists call it the paradoxical element in Marx whereby they trace a trajectory in Marx's thinking that marks a shift from his early "humanist", "moralist" position to a more distinct "materialist" position, its reference point being the notion of praxis. In other words, it was a move from normative to relativist position. The *Paris Manuscripts* (1844), they argue, represents the first position, while *The German Ideology* (1845–46) stands for the second position. Apparently, it sounds paradoxical, if not ambiguous, but they perhaps are right in pointing out that this was a clear indication of Marx's rethinking on the issue of morality.[5] Thus, the so-called problem of paradox or ambiguity can be resolved if it is kept in mind that in Marx's trajectory of thought there was a distinct shift from normativity to relativism, from humanism to historical materialism, from his early concern for the alienated man under capitalism to his search for analysis of capitalism as a production system, from "ought" questions to "is" questions, from man's suffering under capitalism to how capitalism makes man suffer, from philosophy and ethics to political economy, *Capital* being the end-point of this intellectual exercise. The Chinese contribution to this debate provides another interesting clue to the question, namely, why Marx was so scathing in his criticism of the so-called normative questions in philosophy, dismissing them as ideology and espousing thereby a materialist, if not, a relativist position? For the Chinese scholars *The German Ideology* becomes crucial in this context because Marx's agenda in the mid-1840s was to liberate German philosophy from the burden of the past, namely, German idealism, which, for him, was ideology, that had to be unveiled and replaced by the philosophy of the working class, namely, materialism.[6]

This debate on whether Marx espoused any notion of justice or whether he was averse to any moralistic notion like justice becomes especially complicated because Marx has left no canonical text in support of any of these two positions. Consequently, all participants in this debate repeatedly refer to certain representative texts and interpret them from either of these two angles. However, it must be admitted that, while many of his writings are replete with expressions which quite bluntly dismiss the notion of justice as an empty catchword and thereby lend credence to the Wood-Tucker thesis, there is hardly any evidence that shows that Marx categorically defends any normative understanding of justice. This creates a problem for the critics of the relativist position. However, there are two arguments advanced by Nielsen,[7] who is a staunch defender of the normative viewpoint. First, he points out that focusing exclusively on the point that justice, for Marx, is simply relative to the given production relations of society and is thereby historicist presupposes that economic base is the sole determining factor for Marx. What is missing in this understanding is that Marx also recognized the role of superstructure and the active part it plays in affecting the base too. It is in this context that moralistic notions like justice build up their space in Marx's repertory. It is not the framework of linearity but dialectical reciprocity with reference to which the notion of justice in Marx has to be located. This certainly does not mean that Marx espoused any transcendental or transhistorical idea of justice; but it also does not mean that all moral notions like justice are necessarily ideological, these being reflections of the given class relations. In other words, this refers to the age-old question of Marx's recognition of the relative autonomy of the superstructure. As Nielsen explains, especially referring to Marx's *Critique of the Gotha Programme*:

> Marx is *not* telling us that our moral *understanding*, our *understanding* of right and wrong, can never transcend the relations of production we are immersed in; rather he is telling us that the principles of right which will be dominant in a given society will be those of the dominant relations of production of the society in which such principles are articulated. ... That morality is ideology *prone* does not mean that morality is necessarily *ideological*.[8] (Emphasis original)

Second, a number of scholars have quite rightly drawn our attention to expressions used by Marx in his portrayal of capitalist exploitation which are morally loaded. Thus, his description of the capitalist as "thief", "extorter", capitalist profit as "booty", exploitation of the worker as "shameless" and "systematic robbery" is clearly indicative of Marx's very strong moral condemnation of capitalism.[9] His recognition of the importance of the idea of justice is deeply implicit in his texts.

III

Two otherwise somewhat neglected observations of Marx in *Critique of the Gotha Programme* in the context of his famous distinction between the lower and higher phases of communism are of enormous significance in this context. First, in the lower phase, when communism is yet to develop on its own foundations, since it emerges from within the capitalist society, and "is thus in every respect, economically, morally and intellectually, still stamped with the birth-marks of the old society", "*equal right* here is still in principle – *bourgeois right*, although principle and practice are no longer at loggerheads ...".

> The right of the producers is proportional to the labour they supply; the equality consists in the fact that measurement is made with an equal standard, labour. But one man is superior to another physically or mentally and so supplies more labour in the same time, or can work for a longer time; ... This *equal right* is an unequal right for unequal labour. It recognises no class distinctions, because everyone is only a worker like everyone else; but it tacitly recognises the unequal individual endowment and thus productive capacity of the workers as natural privileges. *It is, therefore, a right of inequality, in its content, like every right.*[10] (Emphasis original)

Second,

> In a higher phase of communist society, after the enslaving subordination of the individual to the division of labour, and thereby also the antithesis between mental and physical labour, has vanished; after labour has become not only a means of life but life's prime want; after the productive forces have also increased with the all-round development of the individual, and all the springs of common wealth flow more abundantly – only then can the narrow horizon of bourgeois right be crossed in its entirety and society inscribe on its banners: From each according to his abilities, to each according to his needs![11]

The alternative normativity, worked out in the second formulation, is fully congruent with Marx's position on this question in *Grundrisse*, when he points out:

> In fact, however, when the limited bourgeois form is stripped away, what is wealth other than the universality of individual needs, capacities,

pleasures, productive forces etc created through universal exchange? The full development of human mastery over the forces of nature, those of so-called nature as well as humanity's own nature? The absolute working out of his creative potentialities, with no presupposition other than the previous historic development, which makes this totality of development, i.e. the development of all human powers as such the end in itself, not as measured on a *predetermined* yardstick? Where he does not reproduce himself in one specificity, but produces his totality? Strives not to remain something he has become, but is in the absolute movement of becoming?[12] (Notebook V) (Emphasis original)

Again,

It requires no great penetration to grasp that, where e.g. free labour or wage labour arising out of the dissolution of bondage is the point of departure, there machines can only arise in antithesis to living labour, as property alien to it, and as power hostile to it; i.e. that they must confront it as capital. But it is just as easy to perceive that machines will not cease to be agencies of social production when they become e.g. property of the associated workers. In the first case, however, their distribution, i.e. that they do not *belong* to the worker, is just as much a condition of the mode of production founded on wage labour. In the second case the changed distribution would start from a *changed* foundation of production, a new foundation first created by the process of history.[13] (Notebook VII) (Emphasis original)

This provides a clear outline of the principles that Marx had in mind while working out the idea of an alternative society of the future, based on a new normativity, incorporating the idea of unfettered exercise of free labour, – which alone can accomplish justice in the true sense of the term. Yet, Marx left it as an incomplete, a "radically contingent"[14] understanding of justice, to take the cue from Derrida in *Spectres of Marx*, thus not subscribing to any kind of moral essentialism. It is a spectral vision, unfolding a strange notion of uncertainty, which explains why it struck fear in the minds of the bourgeoisie, since it is not yet known how the alternative face of justice, the alternative normativity would challenge the face of injustice in bourgeois society. Thus, Derrida writes, referring to the situation that prompted the authors of *Communist Manifesto* to refer to the "spectre" of communism that was haunting Europe in the 1840s:

Let us not forget that, around 1848, the First International had to remain quasi-secret. The specter was there ... But that of which it was the specter, communism ... was itself not there, by definition. It was dreaded as communism to come. It had already been announced, with its name, some time ago, but it was not yet *there*. It is only a specter, seemed to say these allies of old Europe so as to reassure themselves, let's hope that in the future it does not become an actual, effectively present, manifest, non-secret reality.[15] (Emphasis original)

IV

Viewed in this perspective, the debate on classical vs normative Marxism loses much of its relevance, since the two notions are dialectically connected. In his search for alternative normativity and in his bid for an alternative notion of justice Marx's take-off point is his relativist understanding of justice in bourgeois society, against which he builds up his normative, yet spectral, vision attainable only under communism. What, however, is most significant is the role of politics which constitutes the element of mediation between these two opposed realms. To take the cue from Lucio Colletti's reading of Rousseau, Marx's idea of transformation of a bad and unjust society into a good and just order was a moral project, but the catalytic element is politics, to be more precise, the politics of fundamental transformation of society, i.e. the act of revolution. The initial step in this direction was taken by Rousseau, when he identified the "ethical task of the triumph of good over evil ... with the political task of the transformation of society".[16] Colletti expands it further, as he says,

> The main consequence of this view of evil as the product of a determinate organization of society is that the problem of the elimination of evil from the world comes to coincide with the problem of revolution. ... The old problem of evil is thus pushed out of the sphere of metaphysics and transferred to the centre of ethics and politics, and turns into the problem of the critique of society, releasing a stimulus of unprecedented power.[17]

This at once provides an interesting twist to Marx's notion of justice. As politics of revolution becomes the mediating factor in the act of transformation of the realm of injustice into that of justice, the instrumentalist understanding of justice is bound to claim relevance. In the name of justice and for the cause of revolution and socialism, violence becomes at times a political and moral imperative, the sanctity of which stands historically justified as a principle. Of course, in working it out in practice, that is, on the operational level if it gets distorted or deformed and for that one has to blame those who act as agents shouldering the responsibility of this project. To be more exact, if violence in the name of revolutionary justice is essentialized without reference to the notion of historicity, it ultimately turns out to be an exercise in instrumentalism.

A careful reading of *Critique of the Gotha Programme*, together with the letter of Engels to August Bebel dated March 18–28, 1875, provides interesting clues to this understanding. In the letter of Engels the political thrust of the future communist society is clarified, when he says that, while the very notion of statism and thereby the Lassallean idea of "free people's state" is incompatible with communism, the transition to communism would necessitate repression of the enemies of the people. But communism would have to free itself from statism, the very notion of the state being associated with force and violence and communism being considered as equivalent to the regime of the common man. To cite Engels,

> Now, since the state is merely a transitional institution of which use is made in the struggle, in the revolution, to keep down one's enemies by force, it is utter nonsense to speak of a free people's state; so long as the proletariat still *makes use* of the state, it makes use of it, not for the purpose of freedom, but of keeping down its enemies and, as soon there can be any question of freedom, the state as such ceases to exist. We would therefore suggest that *Gemeinwesen* be universally substituted for *state*; it is a good old German word that can very well do service for the French "Commune".[18] (Emphasis original)

Marx was much more explicit in his espousal of a transitory state which acts as the agent of revolutionary violence for a higher cause, the cause of communism, when he wrote in *Critique of the Gotha Programme*:

> Between capitalist and communist society lies the period of the revolutionary transformation of the one into the other. Corresponding to this is also a political transition period in which the state can be nothing but *the revolutionary dictatorship of the proletariat.*[19] (Emphasis original)

This, precisely, is the element of historicity which acts as a safety valve against any attempt to essentialize violence in the name of the proletariat.

In sum, Marx's notion of justice is realizable only with reference to revolutionary praxis, which constitutes the mediating element, connecting thereby the two realms of justice, bourgeois and proletarian, false and true, repressive and emancipatory, ideological and moral. While on one level Marx dismisses the possibility of justice in a class society and questions any essentialist, transhistorical and normative understanding of justice, on another level justice is meaningful only under communism, whereby Marx does not negate normativity but projects an alternative normativity in politico-historical as well as moral terms. This involves the crucial revolutionary act of transformation of class society into a regime of equality and freedom, which constitute the core of justice under communism.

Notes

1 For an exhaustive review of this debate see Haroon Rashid, "Making Sense of Marxian Concept of Justice", *Indian Philosophical Quarterly*, XXIX(4), October, 2002, pp. 445–470, Norman Geras, "The Controversy about Marx and Justice", *New Left Review*, (150), March–April, 1985, pp. 47–85 and Norman Geras, "Bringing Marx to Justice: An addendum and Rejoinder",

New Left Review, (195), September–October, 1992, pp. 37–69. The position of Geras is opposed by Wood, as evident in Allen W. Wood, "Justice and Class Interests", *Philosophica*, 33(1), 1984, pp. 9–32. For a very illuminating discussion see Roland Commers, "Marx's Concept of Justice and the Two Traditions in European Thought", *Philosophica*, 33(1), 1984, pp. 107–129. See also Kai Nielsen's two articles, which constituted rebuttal of the positions of Wood and Tucker and affirmation of the "moralist" argument, namely, Kai Nielsen, "The Tucker-Wood Thesis Revisited", *The University of Toronto Law Journal*, 38(1), Winter 1988, pp. 28–63 and "Marx on Justice: A Critique of Marxist Amoralism", *ArchivfuerRechts- und Sozialphilosophie*, 74(1), 1988, pp. 1–32.

2 This has reference to Louis Althusser's essays "On the Young Marx" and "Marxism and Humanism", in *For Marx* (London: Allen Lane, The Penguin Press, 1969).

3 Samuel Freeman (ed), John Rawls, *Lectures on the History of Political Philosophy* (Cambridge, MA: Harvard University Press, 2007), p. 336. To cite Rawls, "Marx did, of course, Condemn Capitalism, but He did so in the Name of Other Values, such as Freedom and Self-realization", p. 338.

4 Ibid., p. 344.

5 Hongmei QU, "Marxism and Morality: Reflections on the History of Interpreting Marx in Moral Philosophy", *Frontiers of Philosophy in China*, 6(2), June, 2011, p. 250.

6 Ibid., p. 255.

7 Nielsen, "The Tucker-Wood Thesis Revisited", pp. 38, 57–58.

8 Nielsen, "Marx on Justice: A Critique of Marxist Amoralism", p. 31.

9 Thomas W. Keys, "Does Marx have a Concept of Justice?", *Philosophical Topics, The Proceedings of the Forty- third and Forty-fourth Annual Meetings of the South Western Philosophical Society* (Spring 1985), p. 284. See also A.M. Shandro, "A Marxist Theory of Justice?", *Canadian Journal of Political Science*, 22(1), March, 1989. He points out, referring to Marx's use of the expressions cited above, that although Marx eschewed the language of justice, his systematic use of these expressions "imply reference to some standard of justice". p. 34.

10 Karl Marx, Frederick Engels, *Collected Works*, vol. 24 (Moscow: Progress, 1989), pp. 85–86.

11 Ibid., p. 87.

12 Karl Marx, *Grundrisse* (Harmondsworth: Penguin Books, 1973), p. 488.

13 Ibid., pp. 832–833.

14 Catherine Kellogg in her article, "The Question of Marx and Justice Revisited: Derrida's Marx and Messianic Time", *Problematique*, (5), 1999, pp. 118–143, distinguishes, following Derrida, between justice as it operates in everyday present and in messianic future, justice present in the acts of injustice in everyday life of class society and justice that is yet to be articulated as a futuristic, ethical vision.

15 Jacques Derrida, *The Specters of Marx* (London: Routledge, 1994), p. 38.

16 Lucio Colletti, *From Rousseau to Lenin. Studies in Ideology and Society* (London: NLB, 1972), p. 144.

17 Ibid., p. 145.

18 Karl Marx, Frederick Engels, *Collected Works*, vol. 24 (Moscow: Progress, 1989), p. 71.

19 Ibid., p. 95.

5 Adequate justice, the fecundity of choice and the interlocutor

Samir Banerjee

Contextualising adequate justice

To contextualise adequate justice perhaps we can begin with an exemplification: the case of animal sacrifice. One might wonder at such a gory illustration. But look closely and one finds that in terms of insight how richly nuanced it is; how it appeals to every human practice: economic, political, cultural, environmental, religious, secular, multicultural-diverse and so on. And it also highlights how fudged the ahimsa/himsa debate can become. In Uttarakhand during certain occasions, buffaloes are sacrificed as a part of the rituals. In earlier periods perhaps due to the paucity of resources these were restricted to a few animals. While it is not clear as to what was done with the carcasses, most probably these were consumed. These days the numbers of such sacrifices, it appears, have multiplied manifold, and at times it seems one can find mounds of carcasses with no takers. Has a practice gone toxic? If so, why? No doubt it is a cruel and violent practice. However, it comes from a past when an animal was sacrificed either to propitiate the Gods, or for consumption or perhaps for both. It could also be because for the farmer the animal was one too many as far as the carrying capacity of the land was concerned. An animal left in the forest to graze would attract carnivores, certainly an avoidable invitation. The best solution was to offer it to the Gods, consume the oblations and in the process if the Gods became happy then so be it. The practice ensured a rhythm between available resources, human consumptions and the environment.

Times have changed and a case is now made that sacrifices should be banned. But how does this impact an individual Uttarakhand farmer? She is encouraged to take up dairy farming. But then she is also restricted from disposing of the surplus and unproductive male and old female/male animals because the law does not readily allow an ox or for that matter a male buffalo to be disposed of. What does she do with unproductive animals particularly when she knows that grazing land in the Himalaya comes at a premium? The entire situation puts her dairy enterprise on the back foot. Her problem is one of relating to the contradictions and conflicts of the system and not violence which she is accused of when she offers an animal for

DOI: 10.4324/9780429355974-5

sacrifice. If one analyses further, we realise that while for a section of society the issue is one of violence, religion and faith, others would want to resolve the conflict of interest involved in making dairy farming a massive capitalist enterprise, while still others would look at it as one of resolving emergent social contradictions inherent in the emerging socio-economic practices. The conflict of interest is particularly deceptive because our farmer is up against inimical forces of which she is not aware. These will systemically and systematically appropriate most of the surplus she generates. Essentially the tension lies in the urge to maximise profits which can lead to failures due to over-competition, falling profits and so-called market mismatch. Rarely will our farmer recognise that under the garb of incentive, initiative and entrepreneurship, her subjectivity will get repressed under the ubiquity of the market – place. As to himsa and ahimsa, the graceful concept of ahimsa is rendered sterile. At the receiving end of the diatribe against himsa because she has to cull her flock, our dairy farmer is perplexed with the faith-induced reach of himsa. Through an articulation of restricting apparent violence, she ends up against the wider problematique of conflicts and contradictions; from man-man conflicts of returns and self-interests to man-nature conflicts of resource mobilisation to a contradiction where the more you succeed, the more you fail! Where does justice come in?

Contradiction is a complex condition. They emerge when our farmer who is certainly knowledgeable about livestock and aspects of animal husbandry is made to think that because of this competence she is also a competent dairy farmer, albeit in the making. The enormous difference between knowing animal husbandry and dairy farming, two distinct processes with some commonalities, get fudged under the facade of incentives, initiatives, entrepreneurship and expectations. She runs into an extremely cruel situation because consequences come later when there is no going back. This predicament is due to the tension between initiative and incentive; initiative is the prerogative of the individual while incentive is a domain of the social. Contradiction thrives in this confusion, and if we may extend it to adequate justice, adequate remains contingent and the real deceptive. To whom does the farmer then turn for justice?

Since the discussion is about justice and Gandhians, a word about ahimsa and satya would be useful. While ahimsa can be understood in many ways, we will take it to mean krodha-tyaag, i.e. renouncing anger. Anger comes from being denied our claims to what we think are our legitimate entitlements and endowments. And tyaag is to give up something to gain or acquire something else or even the same thing through other maybe more appropriate means. A satyagrahi, a martyr or a sanyasi/ascetic renounces only to acquire freedom, spiritual clarity and so on. Ahimsa therefore becomes a paradigm shift wherein anger – a product of denial – is no more the prime motivation. Ahimsa encourages a shift from single-minded personal aggrandisement to a search for truth and a just order, and a sustainable harmony between the personal and the social within us. But while ahimsa helps us reject what we should not want, we still have to articulate what we should want. To revert back to our farmer friend, all she wants is justice and a sustainable socio-economic occupation; not to have to choose from a plethora of conflicts and contradictions. Can she expect adequate justice from society so as to be able to choose a meaningful life? This in turn brings up the issue of satya and whether the individual or society should be responsible to sustain it.

II Violence, conflict, contradictions and judicious choices

An adequate theory is one which should be able to resolve the tension between individual aspirations or interests and the given social reality. Adequacy has to be tested in how well it is able to respond to the often conflicting demands of the processes of social change and continuity. It is in this sense that the term 'adequate' becomes profoundly problematique because of the essential praxis nature of justice which means that although high on principles, justice is always constrained by the nature of society and demands of practice which commends the essential attitude of justice. While on the one hand this signifies a temporal constraint, on the other it begs the question, 'can there be anything which is absolute about justice?' The misleading oft repeated 'law will take its course' or 'the rule of law will prevail' is illustrative of this confusion.

Adequate justice is a temporal incidence. It can mean sufficient or enough for the time or it can mean an adequate response within a given hegemony. This is because justice in society is largely anthropocentric and historic; anything else would mean giving scope for that which is more than human in essence? Further, the adepts who preside over the dispensation of justice don't according to Gandhi put 'truth and service in the first place and the emoluments of the professions in the next place only'? Therefore the question whether justice is to create the condition to give 'freedom from poverty, subjugation, deprivation and so on' and/or is adequate as an adjunct of justice necessary to help 'acquire the freedom to gain the competence to eliminate poverty, subjugation and so on' remains unresolved. In other words is adequate justice the end or the means of liberty from poverty, subjugation, deprivation and so on? But then this is no simple either/or choice. History tells us that the contingency tendency of substantive justice makes this choice problematique. We need to understand why because justice is both a longing and a necessity. This needs some elaboration.

We are all in a hurry; everybody, it seems, wants to arrive, achieve and make a mark; therefore the mantra: 'modernize and assert' to 'flourish and develop'. Further, we are also told we have to change our attitudes, traditions, community norms, dress, eating habits and relationship patterns, just about everything. In effect, *to* progress we have to make judicious choices regarding our society and ourselves. Easy flows the mantra and the promises it makes, and we are left asking, 'What does this mean?' Who is tasked with mediating this change? What are all these various choices? Will this be a transparent participatory engagement? Above all, will the process premised on individual incentive, individual initiative and competition be conflict prone and violent, or harmonious? Perhaps in all this, as history warns us, we might end up with the lawyers laughing all the way to the bank?

Adequate Justice remains a longing for many because in actual practice they remain denied of access to well-being which social living is expected to ensure. Perhaps this is because of a split in the articulation of the spirit of the individual and spirit of the community? In other words this longing is a product of a situation where the spirit of the community seems to serve the interests of only a few? And due to this disparity and varying recompense, some are favoured while most remain left with a sense of longing; for the favoured, adequate justice is a necessity because it then can ensure a sense of stability in social relationships amongst themselves and thus safeguard their hegemony. An upshot of this asymmetry is a possibility that longing and denial can lead to violence and conflict both within and between sections of society. But violence and conflict are not the same. Most of us accept violence as an act and conflict as a relationship. Violence is a one-off act while conflict is a more enduring engagement. This in turn influences our thinking and approach to violence and conflict resolution. Violence, it is insisted, is an assertion, while conflict resolution is a resistance to the conditions which give rise to violence. Violence being a manifestation of a method it is felt can be contained, even used judiciously. Conflict however is more generic. It is a quality embedded in our personal and social discourse: a necessity for a person's social existence. Moreover the import of conflict is always contemporary because it either seeks to ensure hegemony or polemic the establishment. The grammar of violence on the other hand depends upon the immediacy of the issues being contested: land acquisition, alcoholism, rape, caste, wages and so on.

In either case, both violence and conflict evince 'change' as a prerequisite and depend on the context to be able to articulate. At one level we have the urgency of change in the homogenising context of capitalism, modernisation, development and so on; at another level we have to respond to despondency, defencelessness and desperation caused by the change. We see this every day: for some the gospel is the GDP, stock exchange and Wall Street, while for others, it is the struggle against drug trafficking, police atrocities, rape and so on. 'Change', whether for the good or for the bad, is thus the catalyst which engenders both violence and conflict. Sacrificing an animal only postpones conscious, critical and creative critiquing of emerging structures and processes. Paradoxically the act might resolve some of the tension.

In every society change is endemic. To share and reciprocate is post factum to change. An inherent contradiction of change refers to how individuals and communities try to come to grips with the loss of a 'part of the past' in the present, and the 'possibility of losing more' in the future, which forms the *problematique of change and continuity in social transformation*. Sadly appeal to intuitions will not help; nor will impulse and instrumentalism. Democracy, development and modernisation come with violence and conflict and alas also with an element of the inevitable. The inside of every Indian house is reasonably clean. But the outside is astoundingly dirty. Why is this so? Why is the individual's personal ceaselessly in contention with her social? We need to understand the import of this dichotomy. Everybody knows that a dirty environment means infection, suffering and even death. But after knowing why is it that we continue to disregard our own understanding? Is it because we have lost a sense of the community? Is it because family, Panchayat, neighbourhood, our intimate referral points and forums have either become marginalised or perverted? Is it because most of us have no we-feeling for the larger social outside of us in the way it is being articulated? These embedded questions bring us to the more seminal term 'contradiction'. While conflict expresses contradictions, it does not fully explain the significance of contradiction. While conflict is clear about the interests it articulates, contradictions on the other hand signify the potential trauma of false expectations. In the process of recognising these false expectations, the nature of conflict can change, the participants can change and even the original expectations too can mutate. The issue is similar to the distinction between poverty alleviation and poverty elimination; alleviation subtly sustains a given order while elimination replaces it.

III Gandhi and the 'business' of justice

While adequate justice is a vast terrain, our focus will be on how Gandhi and the post-independence Gandhians comprehended this issue and come to terms with social conflicts and contradictions while intervening in the processes of social transformation, i.e. of change and continuity. Intervention here indicates 'associating with the processes of social transformation under circumstances chosen by them'.

Gandhi had always stressed on acquiring the competences to be able to articulate a meaningful social life. He had also recognised that access to such enablement was restricted and that these lead to conflicts and violence. Above all he was aware of the necessity of making judicious choices. In South Africa finding himself in a contradictory position of being a lawyer mediating justice while also being a second class coloured citizen, he was able to comprehend the essential nature of the milieu and his ambiguous position within it. Struggling with these perceptions he scripted the 'Hind Swaraj', which while releasing him from his bondage to lawyer-hood instilled in him a desire to seek abiding social justice, something more than just adequate.

The practice of justice and those of lawyers remains debatable. Chiefly this is because lawyers remain mediators between parties with justice an act of containment first and resolution of causes triggering conflicts coming much later. Gandhi harbouring no illusions about his profession writes,

> Lawyers are also men, and there is something good in every man. Whenever instances of lawyers having done good can be brought forward, it will be found that the good is due to them as men rather than as lawyers. All I am concerned with is to show you that the profession teaches immorality. It is exposed to temptation from which few are saved
>
> (Parel, A; 1997, 59)

and,

> If pleaders were to abandon their profession and consider it just as degrading as prostitution, English rule would break in a day. They have been instrumental in having the charge laid against us that we love quarrels and courts, as fish love water. What I have said with reference to the pleaders necessarily applies to the judge: they are first cousins, and the one gives strength to the other.
>
> (Parel, 1997, 61)

For Gandhi recognising a problem was half the solution. As such he was to write,

> I realised that the true function of a lawyer was to unite parties riven asunder. The lesson was so indelibly burnt into me that a large part of my time during the twenty years of my practice as a lawyer was occupied in bringing about private compromises of hundreds of cases. I lost nothing thereby – not even money, certainly not my soul.
>
> (CW39:11; Parel, 1997, 59)

Thus while recognising the right to justice, cautioning us about agency, particularly an agency whose role is that of a mediator-arbitrator, he reminds us of our duty to remain alert when we outsource to lawyers the task of acquiring justice. Justice is not to be in the giving of anybody. It has to be acquired through conscious involvement. Eulogising the 'means' can mean we will lose the plot to jargons such as 'law will take its course'. For Gandhi, resolution of conflicts and contradictions lies in co-operation, compromise and reciprocation. This is a process of ahimsa wherein harmonious mutuality is a constant aspiration based on truth, a non-negotiable engagement.

While Gandhi spoke a lot about truth he was relatively restrained about justice. Perhaps for him while truth is not in the giving of anybody, justice is in the giving of somebody. For instance justice has to be seen to be done.

Possibly wary of how justice a noun is used more as a verb, adjective or adverb, Gandhi preferred to be cautious. Possibly this could be the reason why he preferred to concentrate on Satya or truth. It is speciously argued that justice is a surrogate sibling of Satya: always in search of its mother. Beyond these a significant point is when Gandhi talks about compromises. Here Gandhi seems to be pointing out the role of three distinct entities in a conflict: the two antagonists and the interlocutor (Nandy, 1992). The inter-locutor presents a narrative, takes a position, will encourage others to pre-sent their views and will dispassionately offer an overview. In Gandhi's view, the role of an interlocutor or satyagrahi is crucial in resolving social conflicts. This is because they never take away the focus from the reasons which create conflicts 'the people' have to live with. He is clear, 'Our salvation can come only through the farmer. Neither the lawyers, nor the doctors, nor the rich landlords are going to secure it' (CWMG, XIII: 214). He explains, 'No one has ever suggested that grinding pauperism can lead to anything else than moral degradation'. For Gandhi the discourse of social justice should begin from grinding pauperism, moral degradation and denial of access.

But the process of acquiring justice however is highly nuanced. As Gandhi puts it, 'Look at the history of the British Empire and the British nation; freedom loving as it is, it will not be a party to give freedom to a people who will not take it to themselves' (CWMG, XIII: 216). Therefore while talking about the interlocutor he warns,

> We want to represent the masses, but we fail. They recognise us not more than they recognise the English Officers. Their hearts are an open book to neither. Their aspirations are not ours. Hence there is a break. And you witness not in reality failure to organise, but want of corre-spondence between the representatives and the represented.
>
> (CWMG, XIII: 221)

During the course of the national movement Gandhi responded to the issues of violence, conflict resolution and contradictions in his own way. Violence for him was to be strictly avoided. At Chauri Chaura he with-drew a movement to protest against the violence which had erupted. In the various Satyagraha, agitations, boycotts and movements such as the Salt Satyagraha, the temple entry movement, boycott of foreign goods and so on, the focus was on conflict resolution. However his stand against separate electoral rolls for those he called Harijan, the 'Trusteeship' concept and his attitude towards technology as distinct from science was more in the nature of responding to social contradictions.

He was against violence because it remains counterproductive. Moreover in society violence has become an art, a discipline and a profession; it has become a highly sophisticated medium in the hands of the elite. The agita-tions against conflict situations such as the taxes on salt, denial of temple entry and boycott of foreign textiles and goods were responses to problems faced by the people. But these agitations did not change the fundamental nature of the social milieu, i.e. the causes remained.

In the separate electoral rolls, the question of technology and the trusteeship concept, he however sought to face essential contradictions. In the electoral rolls issue he realised the fundamental nature of the problem. If the Hindu community was split politically, it would forever remain split. That caste was a pernicious problem could not be denied. That the Hindu community was segregated into tight hierarchic enclaves also could not be denied. But the solution lay in eliminating it rather than give it a permanency by dividing the Hindu community on political lines and that too under colonial rule. The split would only consolidate the division within Hindu society forever. A systemic issue requires systemic solutions. One can agree or disagree with his view; Ambedkar did have a different view.

The Trusteeship issue is less straightforward. Access and control over the economic practice of society are crucial to its well-being. Trusteeship is an engagement with this practice. Two fundamentals are critical to trusteeship: trust, i.e., belief in and reliance on the integrity of a person or institution and its corollary, i.e., the responsibility and obligation placed on a person or institution. Trust therefore becomes the responsibility and obligation reposed on a person or institution, and trusteeship is the function or administrative responsibility of a trustee who holds property for the benefit of others. The critical shift Gandhi made is that for him a trustee consciously and without coercion gives up a traditional, even legal claim of unfettered access and ownership to the benefits of a property and uses it for the benefit of all including his own self. In effect in Gandhi's thinking, while there is room for benevolence, there is none for condescension, charity or coercion.

The idea is to be able to balance endowment and entitlement. However, Gandhi remains wary of accumulation. By stressing on clear normative and moral principles, trusteeship allows every person an opportunity to associate and perform. Gandhi tries to make creation of wealth a means, not an end. Trusteeship should be a mutual pact between the owner and the worker with social good being the principal aspiration. Gandhi accepts the unequal distribution of natural ability amongst people. People are different in terms of natural ability, aspirations, commitment and competence as a consequence of personal and social circumstances and contingencies. Therefore recognising that a human being is more than the system, he seeks to combine incentive, initiative, self-interest and benevolence without giving into state-sponsored dependency or private charity. While trusteeship has been accused of being a bourgeois response to communism, for Gandhi shifting absolute ownership or control and access from the existing owners to many owners or to a bureaucracy and state, or the vanguard and party is no solution. Ownership simply shifts to a coterie. Trusteeship therefore is based on co-operation not collectivisation and is achieved via morally acceptable means such as persuasion and if necessary enlightened non-cooperation where industrialists and landlords refused to see reason.

The other issue which seeks to recognise the contradictions in society is Gandhi's critique of technology. The question is not about Gandhi's attitude towards industrialisation, machinery, consumerism, distribution of wealth and so on, but the impact of all these on all of us as individuals and as a community/society particularly in terms of employment and employability. As a society due to the ingress of technology, we are losing our ways and processes of identifying, locating and nurturing our identities, traditions, culture and independence of aspirations. Centuries of knowledge and wisdom are collapsing and warping.

For Gandhi, 'the ideal of creating an unlimited number of wants and satisfying them seems to be a delusion and a snare'. He was extremely critical of machinery, limitless production and limitless consumption with its attendant illusion of creating leisure and freedom from want. For the interlocutor, at the core of social conflicts and contradictions is accountability, a very discursive notion. And at the core of accountability lies our discretion and commitment in relation to our thoughts and actions. Gandhi acknowledges the necessity of a continuous discourse regarding the why and how of a chosen action being subject to the obligation to report, explains and justifies both to ourselves and to the community. But he simultaneously acknowledges the possibility of a cleavage between choices and results because unlike choice over which we have a measure of control we have very little say over results because results depend upon a wider range of variables. Moreover, since norms and ethics are related to situations, correct interpretation in turn becomes crucial. Hence a healthy understanding of norms and ethics combined with a commitment to make judicious choices in our social discourse ensures accountability.

Secondly, accountability becomes a process of creative engagement and negotiation with the notion of the other as the non-self who, although excluded from, nevertheless defines both our personal and social norms. Interestingly, while our capacity to act is an endowment, our capacity to choose is an entitlement. And these are always mediated by our sense of inadequacy. When we accept this inadequacy and recognise that we cannot fulfil our baggage of expectation in totality, then our desires and choices become attainable and we become accountable to ourselves, and the 'others', too. In Gandhian parlance the issue is sorted out by recognising that your freedom is my limitation and my freedom is your limitation. We become accountable when we strive to take the antagonism out of this predicament. Perhaps in such an understanding of accountability we have a benchmark for adequate justice?

IV Post-independence Gandhian praxis and adequate justice: some experiences

Post-independence social transformation processes became more challenging. The relationship between the oppressor, the oppressed and the interlocutor changed. On the one hand were the state and the professional experts or 'develop-mentalists' who preferred to work with the state, while on the other end were the political revolutionaries who preferred to manage the 'moment' to organise a radical movement and replace the state. In the process Gandhi's hope that 'the state will be there to carry out the will of the people, not to dictate to them or force them to do its will' was quietly ignored.

A noteworthy footnote

At this point a small digression will be useful. In post-independent India, Gandhians were not the only interlocutors who conspicuously and consciously engaged in processes of social change and continuity. Many wanted to influence the course of Indian democracy and ensure justice to all. While the objective was to ensure equal opportunity to all, broadly it focused around development and equitable distribution of the benefits of independence. These interlocutors involving themselves in social work, seekers of justice in social transformation processes were a conspicuous but heterogeneous bloc. They were dubbed '*Jholawallas*' (I use this term with due respect). They carried a '*Jhola*' – a bag which was not a '*Gathari*' – a bundle. Unlike the migrant workers who carried all they owned in a *gathari*, the *jholawalla* – excepting for a small minority – left most valuables with folks back home. And while the haversack was still a novelty, they did not carry a 'briefcase'; these came later as gifts from the funding agencies and the state. Metaphorically the *jhola*, the haversack and the briefcase tell a lot!

The practice of social work remained the central thrust of the *jholawalla* cum activist cum interlocutor. For the post-independence social work fraternity of which the Gandhians were a part, the critical needs which remained dependent on their capacity to choose from amongst alternatives were threefold. Briefly these were first to develop, motivate and create persons who would actively participate and involve themselves in processes of change, which are open-ended, critical and oriented towards creating a future for themselves and their communities. Second, it was to develop linkages between micro, meso and macro levels so that non-hierarchical supportive activities can be generated as and when necessary in the future. Lastly it was to aid in the formulation of hypothesis and implementation of strategies involving three basic objectives: sustainable economics, education, empowerment and organisation building. These formed the essential agenda of the Gandhians and other non-state activists.

In the following section the effort will be to study and comprehend the experience of the above-identified expectations and initiatives through analyses of Khadi gram Ashram, one of the major Gandhian thought-inspired initiatives.

Notes from Khadi gram

Acharya Ramamurti started his involvement in the early 1950s when he quit his lecturer's job at Kashi Vidyapeeth, Varanasi. This was a time of social churning, reorganising and new commitments. Hegemony had passed onto a new order and space had been created which had to be replenished. This was a role waiting for interlocutors.

> Social transformation has to resonate around a voice of truth; a vocali-
> zation which should neither be influenced by a lust for property nor
> intimidated by state authority; a voice which other than a commitment
> towards moral values is neither committed to power nor to any author-
> ity in society. There should be some people who will be the carriers of
> this voice of truth. This is why Gandhi had spoken about the concept
> of Lok Sevak Sangh; the congress should be dismantled and a network
> of Lok Sevaks should spread all over the country. Seven lakh workers
> in seven lakh villages; it was in this context that he had put forth the
> concept of power i.e. generating power, capturing power, and exercis-
> ing power.
>
> (Banerjee S, 2001, 55)

> The workers job is to generate power; People who want to go into poli-
> tics – their job is to capture power. He (Gandhi) said: let the congress
> be an election-fighting machine. (If) they desire to go into politics then
> they should capture power; and exercising power, this is the job of the
> people, let them exercise power. Thus if we understand power in this
> manner then many kinds of difficulties are resolved; and every one of
> us must decide about power, i.e. in relationship to power what is our
> position. Accordingly the role of an activist becomes very clear in that
> our role is that of generating power.
>
> (Ibid, 55)

The worker here is the activist/social worker/interlocutor.

This distinction regarding power is crucial to non-violent collective action. To elaborate the approach has four distinct implications: the first is the urge and also the necessity to intervene in the processes of social trans-formation; the second is the relation with the state; third is the distinctness and import of the family as a unit to all interventionists as individuals; lastly is the necessity to distinguish the dual meaning of institution – an organisa-tion or establishment and a well-established pattern of behaviour or rela-tionships, for instance the ashram and the Gandhian ethos. Accordingly for Ramamurti,

> The basic problem of this country is democracy; because democracy
> means that unless people acquire that strength which helps them

recognize their rights and that which helps them recognize their duties, then this bureaucratic state will subjugate them. ... all the other work that we do in the name of development should be considered to be relief work only. Such [development work] will not bring about any basic change. [It] will not bring any changes in the policies of the state.

(Banerjee S, 2001, 15)

Therefore in independent India, violence, conflict resolution and resistance have to be within the context of democracy. Hence within the Gandhian paradigm Ramamurti distinguishes four fundamental elements in any resistance: the need for an enlightened engagement, the necessity and role of an interlocutor, the necessity of concrete intervention programmes and the site of actual intervention. Democracy promises 'true' living, but it remains eclectic to Socrates' question 'How should I live?' Moreover like Kant it tends to suggest that happiness is the antithesis of virtue. However, democracy allows scope to reclaim one's self-esteem, and unlike utopia it takes into account the empirical, the personal initiative and in particular it revels in the day-to-day critical creativity of society. While in its pristine form it abjures certitude in practice, it remains dialectic bound and therefore barely a step beyond certitudes.

For Acharya Ramamurti the question of democracy and intervention as resistance to the issue is one of self-realisation. And,

In this age, Gandhi's concept of self-realization could be seen as the most serious effort to locate within the individual and in action the subject-object dichotomy (man as the maker of history versus man as the product of history; man as a self-aware aspect of nature versus man as a product of biological evolution; the ego or reality principle versus the id or pleasure principle; praxis versus dialectic or process).

(Nandy, 1992, 36)

V Self-realisation as social work

The parameter Ramamurti identifies covers a wide range of issues and implications. For our part we will focus on some crucial aspects related particularly to the activists' personal and social engagements as experienced and understood by Ramamurti and his colleagues. The 'voice of truth' is obviously related to the question of the role of the interlocutor. To this should be added another decidedly crucial insight which Ramamurti elaborates:

We are here (in a village near Jamui, Bihar involved in developmental activities) because we want to be here; not that people want us to be here. But we want to be here. This makes a lot of difference. Today if it can be said about the poor people we served for forty years, they will certainly say that we should stay and not go away. But if we went away they will not lose anything. It is alright, people came because they wanted to and they have gone because they wanted to.

He is in effect telling us that while they were stakeholders in the nation-building transformation processes, they still needed to acquire such stakes at the local level. This relationship with the people is a site more elemental than the overarching national. Social well-being is neither an endowment nor an entitlement of any group or individual to distribute to others. The mutuality of the activist-interlocutor and the beneficiary people has to emerge. While the activist engages with the will the community sustains the soul. Hiatus in this can lead to profound disconnect. Today Jamui district is heavily influenced by the Naxalite movement and ideology.

However, the parallel local and national processes of liberal democracy continue. Whose then is the 'voice of truth'? The problem is with this notion of truth. The problematique is because truth holds distinct philosophical, moral and pragmatic quotidian connotations. For Gandhi 'truth' involves elements of theory and practice. It carries a lot of conceptual baggage and is more than the common sense usage. Therefore while Gandhi might have suggested that all activities must be premised on truth, we still have to define 'truth' for itself. Moreover, 'truth' by itself does not evaluate success or failure. Truth can only caution us, particularly against exclusivity. However, truth can help us establish a harmonious relationship between the personal and the social, two perpetually contending facets of our individual being. Obviously Satyagraha, non-violence and a deep sense of plurality help us mediate this involvement with truth.

Very simply, truth is the process of recognising one's potential both as an individual and as a social being to not just fulfil our destiny but to understand the destiny itself. When Gandhi revises the standard formula 'God is truth' to read 'truth is God', he in effect is saying that the individual (all individuals) is divine. But this insight is not in the giving of anybody because this insight is a matrix of happiness and morality unlike knowledge is wisdom. 'Voice of truth' therefore is the ethical yearning audible to the seeker – activist.

Another problematique is that of the family and the internal conflict which the activist has to deal with due to the demands the family retains and expects. The interlocutor joins a movement or an institution/ashram thereby hobbling his/her ambitions. The decision is that of the individual activist. The family has no role in this decision. Ramamurti observes:

We made a decision and we came here. This was not a decision of our wives or our children. They came because we came. They grew up and they started thinking. They became perplexed about their plight. This led to a split; a split, which Gandhi tried to resolve at Sabarmati ashram and Sevagram ashram. But he did not succeed.

(Banerjee S, 2001, 41)

This split is to indicate the evolving nature of agency where the individual, the family and the neighbourhood all compose and recompose the agency of social transformation. While replacement of the family as the fundamental unit with an organisation as the primordial unit remains problematique, debunking just avoids the issue altogether. And the consequence every activist knows is generally unfortunate to say the least; either the operation suffers or the activist gives up or the state uses the family to neutralise the activist and their activity.

A third implication Ramamurti explains is due to 'an uncritical acceptance of the state for material and moral sustenance', while ignoring the states' fundamental class-centric nature. After the 1975 emergency the state was able to marginalise if not dismantle many Gandhian institutions. Most of this was because the institutions for their outreach programmes which established their links with the people had become over-dependent on state largesse. While partly this was due to the Gandhians' past association with the congress party, it was also due to an uncritical acceptance of the role of the state. This of course began with a benign shift towards the individual activist as the agency for resistance and transformation. Ramamurti reminisces that 'We' as servants of the people thought that we had become one with the people, but then 'servants of the people' in a democracy is enigmatic, a problem the Gandhians did try to come to grips with in a post-Gandhi seminar (Gandhi Gopalkrishna and Snell Rupert, 2007).

Fourthly we have the problematique of the structures of intervention – the institution. The ashram with its slogan of self-sufficiency by trying to replace the village which for all concerned is an institution by itself created a split in loyalty. It was particularly confusing because while the village was expected to continue with the traditional, the new institute would take over the responsibility for change and transformation. This split is very difficult to negotiate particularly because the ashram as an agency is reluctant to accept the hegemony of the village as an institution. Empowerment apparently begins with allegiance and preferably at home, that is the Ashram.

Ramamurti explains this observable fact while explaining the failure of the 'shramshala' school initiative where the student while learning reading, writing and arithmetic had to spend time labouring in the fields, cleaning toilets, etc. This initiative was in line with Gandhi's understanding of bread labour. But the people were not convinced. As far as they were concerned, 'doing this (labour) has reduced us to this condition. Now we are once again being asked to do the same all over again'. The *shramshala* school initiative failed.

Besides working through an institution, Ramamurti and many of his colleagues worked with another couple of people-oriented approaches. The first was the various ashram-based employment-related activities and the constructive programme which can be described as general, ethical and contemplative. These were put together as an import of the age, spirit of the era, message of the epoch and so on. Together, these had an enhancing impact. The second is what Ramamurti calls 'thrust' endeavours, namely, *Panchayat*, i.e. local self-government and *Padosiat*, i.e. neighbourhood. Panchayat is an age-old institution where five village elders, usually men, helped resolve village issues and problems on the basis of local traditions and aspirations. Padosiat or neighbourhood refers to a contagious region over which people interacted in terms of economics, politics and culture. This essentially contoured the individual's memories and history. Together these two indicate for Ramamurti the personal and the social agenda of the activist.

Essentially the thinking behind these concepts is based on the assumption that no activist can live in an exclusive location where transformation is restricted to the local. In today's world globalisation is all pervading. This globalisation is further complicated by it being a 'globalisation of federal nations' where the nation itself is not homogenous. And above all, links sustaining this are firmly the hegemony of certain powers, their associates and surrogates. For the local people the only way to restrain this hegemony is through the Panchayat with its focus on local political and economic practices and an overarching neighbourhood stressing culture, ethics, history, spiritual and so on. Together they have the potential of creating a sense of locality as a counterpoint to the centralising tendency of nationalism and globalisation. The Panchayat system is amiable to local initiative which is easily discernible. While it is influenced by individualism, elitism, family connections and cronyism, it is also the irreducible site of social struggles between contending forces represented by the state and the people. While power for the state stems from obedience, sanction and repression, for the masses it emerges from *informed association and self-reliance*. The Panchayat as a forum to debate the well-being of all, starting from the local, has the potential of aiding this informed association. Padosiat is a larger platform. Nation as a concept is overtly political. The concept of neighbourhood tries to rectify this bias because conflict resolution based only on a political agenda, particularly in a democracy open to forces of globalisation, is unsustainable. Analyses of recent movements, uprisings and so on conclusively show this. The problem is unlike a village Panchayat the boundaries of a neighbourhood are indistinct and liable to overlap. In many ways it stands for sharing within a region without compromising on differences. While a Panchayat is mandated to resolve economic, political and such other problems, the Padosiat is something like a watershed where the focus is on accommodating various mobilisation patterns; uphill the grazer focuses on the grass and is bothered about inundation while downhill along the same river the farmer seeks to impound some of the water so as to irrigate his fields. Both have to recognise that percolation and inundation are two sides of the same coin.

VI Tracking resistance

Perhaps we can summarise and highlight some of the more significant les-
sons regarding the experiences and insights gained in terms of action and
agency from the ashram-based constructive programme and the *Panchayat*
and *Padosiat*-based *thrust* activities.

The first issue obviously refers to the role of the human agency as individual or group in effectively intervening in social transformation processes.
Ramamurti spoke of a voice of truth and he also recognises that such a
voice has always existed. But from whom does this voice emerge? Will
it be from amongst the local people or will it be from an import? Will it
be from amongst the landless peasant, the proletariat or the intellectuals?
The issue is further complicated by the enormous influence of family, sect,
caste and so on. One thing however is clear, the community expects that
such voices must explicitly associate with the community, abjure opportun-
ism and search for inspirations and incentives from and on the basis of an
organic linkage with the community and not be a tutored engagement of
the elite. Moreover intervention of such voices should emphasise enablement. Intervention should be mutually arrived enablement and not some
borrowed assurances.

Second, social movements seek to mobilise power, and this mobilisation has a moral element within it. For Ramamurti the people exercise
power while the activists and the politicians generate and capture power
respectively. The hold over power becomes precarious when the activist
and politician is the same, or belong to the same power bloc and gang up.
In a democracy the onus then shifts away from the people with the politician and the activist claiming to 'serve' the people. Ramamurti is suggesting inclusiveness and the contours of this inclusivity can be mapped
through Panchayat and *Padosiat*. Interestingly both concepts have an
enormous moral appeal particularly in rural India. This morality incidentally refers to Gandhi's triad of rights and duties, means and ends and
needs and wants.

The struggle for independence created an ethos which gave primacy to
the political. When the struggle for independence ended, a reorientation
became necessary. The first of all engagement was on what comes first: the
new nation or the old community – civilisation. The new Indian nation state
is a complex nomenclature. While in terms of culture it resonates well with
the past and appeals to the people, its proposed political and economic practices come straight from the boardrooms of the elite. Against this hegemony
the ashram-centred construction programme along with Panchayat and
Padosiat offers a meaningful participatory alternative. This however has
to negotiate a difficult terrain. The new elite if anything is ambitious. India
as a new nation allows them a lot of liberty to re-contour existing social
relationships and overall aspirations of the social formation as a whole.
The privileging of the political over other human practice and 'we are the

servants of the people' slogan of the politician-activist creates a mystifying ethos wherein self-interest of self-servers remains concealed. Consequently while transparency became a casualty, focus shifts from autonomy and dialogue to delivery; and delivery ensures a shift from inclusive to the exclusive. Soon the community becomes the recipient. To ensure delivery the state creates a dichotomy between ends and means. Both ends and means henceforth become the domain of the state. For this the community has to be subservient to the nation. With state power this is possible because the emergent elite can legitimately use violence and thereby assert its will.

But the fledgling emergent state did not have the resources to ensure its will. Large swathes of rural India remained outside the 'Delhi centred development-modernization discourse'. This is where the Gandhian came in. Imbued with a sense of sarvodaya the interlocutors attracted to the ashrams were either idealists or remnants of the national movements. The task of nation building was not going to be easy. Adding confusion to all this was caste, class, the growing aspiration of the elite and an ambiguous national identity vis-a-vis regional identities. In all this the local became the first casualty and obviously a concern of the Gandhian. A space for intervention emerged, but it came with its problems. On the one hand they had to respond to the local while on the other dialogue with the new garrulous 'development-modernization discourse'.

Constraints, spontaneity and certitude are elemental to social mobilisation. But the significance of these has to be learned in context of the specific. In practice Panchayat soon became an instrument of the political elite and state administration. As local self-government it became an appendage of the parliamentary system. Between the BDO and the Panchayat secretary both government official and the sarpanch, a politician, very little remains for people's initiative. However, it still retains the distinction of being the forum of first appeal/initiative through which people can relate with each other, dialogue and plan their lives. Moreover unlike the state assemblies and the national parliament it has no space for grandstanding because the self-interest of the participants is clearly discernible to all. A Panchayat can be manipulated, threatened, overruled and subjugated, but it cannot be fooled.

Padosiat on the other hand was to articulate the community civilisation linkage. In today's milieu this can easily mean overlapping of state and national boundaries. Assam, Bangladesh, West Bengal, eastern parts of Bihar and Odisha can easily form a congenial neighbourhood for they have a lot of synergy. Parts of Marathwada, Telangana and Karnataka adjacent to each other have many commonalities and can interact profitably as a common neighbourhood. But this militates against national and state boundaries while the second impinges upon linguistic boundaries. Thirdly we have this problematique of the activist's family relationship. Family is not just where an individual and partner together beget progeny. In many ways it is the fundamental unit of care. It is this care which Ramamurti and many of his colleagues have been trying to project: care of the individual through the family, care of the village through the Panchayat and care of the community civilization through the Padosiat. But then the family is made up of independent individuals, and in a democracy an individual is paramount. The individual has to understand that care has to be nurtured by compromise, i.e. the individual's compromise with the community.

To sum up, Panchayat and Padosiat can redefine the thrust of democracy by modifying the engagement between state and civil society by encouraging an element of autonomy. If this shift happens, the individual and the family can broad base its civil concerns beyond the narrow political. Consequently instead of depending on institutional state power, people can pursue their varied aspirations by mobilising at the local level. The means and ends of assertion of authority and delivering governance can then become genuine peoples' responsibility. After all, communication between people cannot be a state responsibility. The fundamental problem in this is the notion of development itself where the state and the elite remain the philosopher, judge, jury and policeman. The state has to focus on enabling and stop being the great mentor, monitor. It has to stop telling everybody to sustain development while retaining the exclusive authority to define development. Can the people also have a right to recover their own definition of needs as against the wants which development seems to foist on them? Ramamurti and his colleagues did offer some insights. And as far as he was concerned: 'whether we succeeded or not, the nation will have to judge'.

Involvement begins with acknowledging the mutuality and the nurture one can provide another, not in exchange for what the other can or has done, but as reciprocation for the overall nurture one receives. It presupposes a vision for oneself, for society, and a way in accordance with which one could transform society. In Gandhian parlance this vision of involvement is sarvodaya, 'Welfare of All'. In sarvodaya, involvement cannot be a sporadic reaction to a situation. It has to be a constructive effort, which should be need based and not interest or wants based. Since sarvodaya takes Satyagraha, swaraj and swadeshi as its practice, involvement as sarvodaya becomes a *sadhana*, and a means of accomplishing self-knowledge. And, as one grows in self-knowledge, it becomes a spontaneous and natural expression of one's own self. Sarvodaya therefore is never just a project.

Involvement and therefore sarvodaya is an engagement with four issues: mediating the relationship between the personal, the family and the social; the question of Social transformation, development and state; the role of non-state forums in social transformation; the means and ends conundrum. To illustrate, why for instance is there an element of coercion in the relationship between the individual, the family and society? It is because the relationship is rarely transparent and there are hidden agendas. The same holds for development and the development expert. On the other hand the role of the state is clear wherein for those in hegemony want is a basic need.

This in turn means moving from the more ethical attribute of involvement to pragmatic aspects of intervention which presupposes motives and intentions. Social intervention seeks mediation along certain lines. The problem is with selecting an approach because some arguments (and every argument will have some takers) can negate at least some aspects of any and every orientation and worldview. The only thing that cannot be negated is one's own self. Not surprisingly, since leadership is a crucial element in intervention, Gandhi's focus was the self that is the individual, and not some vanguard, elite or proletariat; and certainly not on an exemplar who will lead to *Gandhigiri* or as the media would have it, 'a brand'.

Gandhian thought gives primacy to action. And action is to be chosen on the basis of its being desirable. The problem is in defining 'desirable'. One way is to describe it at three levels; the first is how inclusive it is in terms of involvement; the second refers to the comprehensiveness of the action in terms of taking into account all factors, implicit and explicit that constitute the action; and lastly how it measures up to the issue of consequences. Above all, the worth of an action should be judged by the goodness of the consequent state of affair. All social actions are mediated events which end up as consequences, and over a period merge to give scope for further action. Veritable action, events and consequences continuously unfold. Therefore, all desirable actions are those which establish goodness in the milieu, which they influenced and are contingent upon. Social intervention thus becomes Satyagraha.

Interlocutors don't solve the problems. They only enable the people to seize the occasion. Every chapter of the book they edit has to be a narrative by the people. While the interlocutor writes the prologue, the epilogue remains dialogical. Their involvement is necessary, but never sufficient. They can create the competence to seek adequate justice, but acquiring justice has to be an act of tyaag: give up something to acquire something. This holds for the interlocutor as well as the people.

Bibliography

Banerjee Samir (2001) *Bas Eak Kadam Aur*, Hindi, Indian Institute of Advanced Study, Shimla.

Banerjee Samir and Ghotge Sanjeev (ed. 2001) *Contributions towards an Agenda for India*, Indian Institute of Advanced Study, Shimla.

Banerjee Samir and Namra Aman (ed. 2001) *Sangathan, Shaktivardan Aur Gandhi Vichar*, Hindi, Indian Institute of Advanced Study, Shimla.

Banerjee Samir (2009) *Notes from Gandhigram: Challenges to Gandhian Praxis*, Orient Blackswan, New Delhi.

The Collected Works of Mahatma Gandhi, *(CWMG), 90 vols.* Publication Division of the Government of India, Navajivan, New Delhi, 1958–84.

Gandhi Goplakrishna and Snell Rupert (ed. 2007) 'Gandhi is Gone', in *Who Will Guide Us Now*, Permanent Black, Ranikhet.

Hardiman David (2003) *Gandhi in His Time and Ours*, Permanent Black, Delhi.

Nandy Ashis (1992) 'Towards a Third World Utopia', in *Traditions, Tyranny and Utopia*, Oxford University Press, Delhi.

Parel Anthony (ed. 1997) *Gandhi: 'Hind Swaraj' and other Writings*, CUP, Delhi.

Parel Anthony (ed. 2000) *Gandhi, Freedom and Self-Rule*, Vistaar Publications, Delhi.

S C Biswas (ed. 1990) *Gandhi: Theory and Practice, Social Impact and Contemporary Relevance*, Indian Institute of Advanced Study, Shimla.

Sachs Wolfgang (ed. 1997) *The Development Dictionary*, Orient Longman, New Delhi.

6 Outline of a postcolonial theory of justice[1]

Partha Chatterjee

I

> *Transcendental theories that define the universally valid institutional forms of a perfectly just society are inappropriate.*

The famous social contract theories that have long shaped normative ideas of the modern state are founded on universal assumptions regarding human nature. They also insist that their conclusions regarding the perfectly just society must command complete agreement since they follow irresistibly from those assumptions by the application of universal principles of reason. The contract-based theories of justice of Hobbes, Locke and Rousseau all share this feature. But it is clear from the historical evidence since the seventeenth century that no actual human society of the modern world ever displays such universal characteristics of human nature, nor can it ever arrive at complete agreement over the fundamental principles of justice. The actual problem of ensuring justice in modern societies cannot be adequately tackled by transcendental theories of the universal institutions of a perfectly just society.

Since statements have sometimes been made about the perfectly just socialist or communist society, it is worth remembering that Marx strongly resisted such transcendental institutional theories in his *Critique of the Gotha Programme* (1875).[2] Thus, he insisted that communist society must be thought of "not as it has *developed* on its own foundations, but, on the contrary, just as it *emerges* from capitalist society ... still stamped with the birthmarks of the old society". An example of this is "equal right" in communist society which, Marx says, will still remain bourgeois right and equivalent exchange will exist only on the average and not in each individual case. "Right can never be higher than the economic structure and its cultural development conditioned thereby." In short, communist society is to be described not in terms of transcendental conceptions of the perfectly just society but historically and comparatively.

Gandhi often described the perfect society as one in which political power operating through representatives would become redundant.

DOI: 10.4324/9780429355974-6

Representatives will become unnecessary if the national life becomes so perfect as to be self-controlled. It will then be a state of enlightened anarchy in which each person will become his own ruler. He will conduct himself in such a way that his behaviour will not hamper the well-being of his neighbours. In an ideal State there will be no political institution and therefore no political power.[3]

For India, he described the perfectly just society as *rāmarājya*, a patriarchy in which the ruler, by his moral quality and habitual adherence to truth, always delivers justice.[4] In *rāmarājya*, the economic organization of production, arranged according to a perfect fourfold *varṇāśrama* scheme of specialization and a perfect system of reciprocity in the exchange of commodities and services, always ensures that there is no spirit of competition and no differences in status between different kinds of labour.[5] Nevertheless, despite his lifelong adherence to his transcendental conception of the perfect society, Gandhi never expected that there would be universal agreement on this ideal or even that he himself would be able to live up to its principles.[6] Indeed, he chose the path of politics to bring about through persuasion and popular mobilization the conditions for greater social justice.

There are also religious conceptions of the perfectly just society based on the revealed word of god. Needless to say, transcendental theories based on religious doctrine can find acceptance only among those who profess faith in that particular interpretation of the religion. They can be made to apply to non-believers only by the application of force.

II

The comparative approach to justice based on actual practices prevailing in different societies deserves serious attention.

Rejecting transcendental institutionalism, Amartya Sen has argued for a comparative approach to justice that grounds itself in the actual behaviour of people and acknowledges the relevance of global perspectives.[7] Since justice depends on a combination of institutional features and the actual behaviour of people, just institutions can only be defined by making them contingent on actual behaviour (which is not the same as just or reasonable behaviour, since real people can often be unjust or unreasonable). A comparative and historical approach to justice must recognize that one cannot define a set of universal principles of justice (say, in a philosophical treatise or even a lawfully proclaimed constitution) and expect everyone to fall in line. Sen argues that one must approach justice through comparisons between different social states, consider the social consequences of institutional rules, recognize the incompleteness of social preferences while providing guidance for the removal of injustice and note the voices of those who were not part of the actual process that created the institutions of justice (such as the constitution). Sen also argues that in the modern world, no discussion of justice can ignore examples and precedents from other parts of the world, even if they are rejected. The comparative approach to justice must include a global perspective.[8]

Basing his arguments on theories of social choice, Sen does provide an influential comparative approach to the question of justice. However, his theory is insufficiently specified. In this chapter, I will argue that in seeking to build a more adequate comparative and historical theory of justice for postcolonial societies, Sen's arguments must be substantially modified and extended in other directions.

III

The basic conceptual apparatus for a globally applicable comparative theory of justice, based on the procedure of normalization, was provided by utilitarian thinkers of the early nineteenth century.

The conceptual innovations that made possible a comparative theory of justice with a global perspective appeared only around the turn of the nineteenth century. By then, European countries had had the experience of conquering and ruling over vast territories in the Americas. But the European empires in the Western hemisphere never seriously posed the problem of having to incorporate within a European political order the forms of law, property and government of the indigenous American peoples. The latter were not regarded as having a credible political society at all that needed to be integrated into the new imperial formation. In fact, the indigenous societies of the Amerindian peoples frequently served as examples of the pre-political natural condition of mankind that had to be superseded for the political and commercial societies of civilized people to emerge. (Recall Locke's dramatic assertion on the origins of property in land: "Thus in the beginning all the World was *America* ...".)[9] But the European conquests in Asia that began in the second half of the eighteenth century posed entirely different problems. The existing political institutions of those defeated Oriental kingdoms could not be entirely set aside, for utterly real political reasons. They had to be given a place within the new imperial order of European rule over its Eastern colonies. Thus began a new journey of normative Western political theory.

Writing his *Principles of Morals and Legislation* in 1789, Jeremy Bentham declared that the methods and standards of legislation he was proposing were "alike applicable to the laws of all nations".[10] More interestingly for us, in an early essay on "The Influence of Time and Place in Matters of Legislation", Bentham proposed the following method:

I take England, then, for a standard; and referring every thing to this standard, I inquire, what are the deviations which it would be requisite to make from this standard in giving to another country such a tincture as any other country may receive without prejudice from English laws. ... The problem, as it stands at present, is – the best possible laws for England being established in England, the variations which it would be necessary to make in those of another given country, in order to render them the best laws possible with reference to that other country.[11]

In providing an instructive example of this method, Bentham chose a country that presented "as strong a contrast with England as possible".

> Such a contrast we seem to have in the province of Bengal. Climate, face of the country, natural productions, present laws, manners, customs, religion of the inhabitants; every circumstance on which a difference in the point in question can be grounded, as different as can be. ... To a lawgiver, who having been bred up with English notions, shall have learnt how to accommodate his laws to the circumstances of Bengal, no other part of the globe can present any difficulty.[12]

But Bentham also insisted that "human nature was everywhere the same" and that different countries did not have "different catalogues of pleasures and pains". Then why should not the same laws hold good for all countries? Because the things that caused pleasure or pain were not the same everywhere. "The same event ... which would produce pain or pleasure in one country, would not produce an effect of the same sort, or if of the same sort, not in equal degree, in another."[13] But these grounds of variation were not all of the same kind either. Some were physical, such as the climate or the nature of the soil, and these were invariant and insurmountable. Others, no matter how difficult or inexpedient, were subject to intervention and change, such as "the circumstances of government, religion, and manners".[14] Different sets of laws would be appropriate for different circumstances. Further, by the application of appropriate laws, the mutable circumstances could be subjected to the forces of change.

Bentham thought of these variations as amenable to more or less precise and detailed qualitative and quantitative comparison – that is to say, they were all subject to some common measure. He suggested that the legislator should be provided with two sets of tables relating to the country for which he was legislating. One set would consist of the civil code, the constitutional code, a table of offences and punishments, etc. and the other set would comprise tables of the moral and religious biases of the people, a set of maps, a table of the productions of the country, tables of the population, and the like.[15] Armed with these, he would be able to devise the best possible laws for any country.

Reading Bentham today, one can almost imagine an anticipation of the statistical handbooks of social indicators with which any undergraduate of the twenty-first century is now able to rank the countries of the world according to standards of living, mortality rates, quality of governance, human development and dozens of other evaluative criteria. Unlike in the writings of eighteenth-century historians and travellers brought up on Montesquieu, cultural difference here is no longer incommensurable. Rather, it can now be seen in terms of its consequences, plotted as deviations from a standard and hence normalized. Governments everywhere have been brought within the same conceptual field. All deviations between states were now comparable according to the same measure. States could be divided into ranks and grades. Justice, in other words, has been normalized and made comparable across the world.

Moreover, once normalized, deviations could be tracked over time: the deviation of a state from the norm could close or widen. Thus, in time, a country could conceivably enter the grade of "advanced societies" or drop out of it. The important innovation here was the handle that was afforded for the intervention of "policy" to affect the distance of an empirical state from the desired norm. Indeed, as the philosopher Ian Hacking has shown, the statistical elaboration of the idea of normality in the nineteenth century would establish two senses of the norm: one, the normal as the right and the good – the normative, as political philosophy, for instance, would have it – and the other, the normal as the empirically existent average or mean, capable of improvement.[16]

IV

Normalization provides the techniques for relating the normative to the empirical.

The significance of this conceptual innovation for the emergence of new practices of government in the nineteenth and twentieth centuries has not been adequately stressed. We see the concepts elaborated for the first time in Jeremy Bentham and his "utilitarian" theories of legislation. But these formal properties of the comparative method would become part of the background assumptions of virtually all modern schools of thought on the subject of justice, including many that had no truck with the baggage of utilitarianism as a political philosophy. Notwithstanding Bentham's exaggerated confidence in the ability of his method to provide exact and unimpeachable solutions to every policy problem, what it did mark out was a conceptual field that could in principle integrate into a single theoretical domain all questions of governance in every society that exists in the world. Its comparative method of normalization would establish an enduring modality of relating the domain of the normative to that of the empirical, something that would long outlast the limited appeal of utilitarian political philosophy. The norm-deviation structure has provided, from the nineteenth century to the present day, an enduring framework for addressing policy questions of improvement, progress, modernization and development.

However, Bentham's comparative method would also establish a second global paradigm. If constitutionally established representative government was to be recognized as the universally valid normative standard, then the universally valid and legitimate exception to that norm could only be some form of enlightened despotism. Despotism is unlimited and arbitrary power, unconstrained by constitutional rules. In this sense, it was often distinguished in the classical literature of the seventeenth and eighteenth centuries from absolutism which was unlimited power but legitimately constituted within certain fundamental laws. The form of government recommended by the new normative theory for European colonies in the East was absolutist in the sense that while it did not recognize any limits to its sovereign powers within the occupied territory, it did claim to be constituted by, and to function within, certain fundamental laws. But it was despotic in its foundational assumptions since the authority that was to lay down those fundamental laws was arbitrarily constituted and not in any way responsible to those whom it governed. But when despotism claims to be enlightened, it places a limit on itself and promises to itself to be responsible: it becomes limited by and responsible to enlightened reason. When that happens, there is effectively no difference between despotism and absolutism. Despotism has to justify its actions to itself by their results.[17] Since the empirically prevailing average social conditions in the "backward" colonies were different from those in the advanced countries, the normative standard of the latter would have to be altered to suit the former. The universally valid norm would have to be withheld in favour of a colonial exception.

This structure of norm and exception can be seen in virtually every justification of colonial empires in the nineteenth and twentieth centuries. The puzzle posed by postcolonial political theory – by Uday Singh Mehta, for example – of liberal-democratic governments of Europe holding overseas territories under their despotic rule, thus apparently contradicting their cherished normative principles, dissolves when one realizes the power of the norm-exception construct.[18] Thus, John Stuart Mill, one of the greatest liberal political theorists of all time, while making an extended case for the universal superiority of representative government, specifically argued that it could not apply, at least not yet, to dependencies such as India.[19] The latter were exceptions; hence there was really no contradiction in Mill's normative liberal theory. He recommended a paternal British despotism for those countries, until such time as their peoples became mature enough to govern themselves. Of course, neither Mill nor any other liberal could suggest an impartial way of deciding when and if such a stage had been reached. Apparently, there was no alternative but to rely on the good sense of the paternal guardians to grant self-government to their wards. Or rather, the only alternative was to acknowledge the right of a subject people to announce its attainment of maturity by rebelling against its masters – a right incompatible with liberal doctrines of good colonial governance.

From the nineteenth century, therefore, the two senses of the norm encoded the basic political strategy of relating the normative to the empirical. The norm-deviation structure would establish the empirical location of any particular social formation at any given time in relation to the empirically prevailing global average or normal. The corresponding normative framework could then provide, by means of a norm-exception structure of justification, the ground for the application of "policy" to intervene and bring the empirical average closer to the desired norm. Normalization was the theoretical key to this political strategy.

The norm-deviation method as a crucial aspect of modern disciplinary practices is, as Michel Foucault has shown, ubiquitous in the operations of the modern regime of power.[20] The norm-exception formula too, as I will show below, is used widely to deal with the exigencies of heterogeneity and uncertainty in a policy field that has been presumably normalized. What I am also suggesting through my thumbnail sketch of the conceptual history of political institutions in the modern West is that, contrary to the long enshrined received narrative, those institutions and their normative principles were not the products of an exclusively endogenous development but the result of Europe's encounters with its colonial territories, first in the Americas and then in Asia and Africa. It is this intellectual history of the comparative approach to government that opens up the possibility of a specifically postcolonial theory of justice.

V

The problems of interpersonal comparisons of utility that were germane to utilitarian theory have been circumvented by recent theories of social welfare that seek to reconcile rational behaviour as a normative order with the actual behaviour of people showing different degrees of rationality.

Social choice theory grew out of attempts by nineteenth-century mathematicians to devise the best possible rules of collective decision-making in bodies such as committees or juries. As Hacking has shown, this approach led to a quite novel form of reasoning based on the probabilistic estimation of uncertain outcomes – a method entirely different from the deterministic approach of conventional scientific thinking.[21] Alongside this development, questions were raised about the tenability of making comparisons of utility between different persons who did not share the same ordering of preferences between different choices. How could all individual preferences be reduced to a common measure of utility and summed up as a social choice? In more technical language, the two major problems with classical utilitarianism were interpersonal comparison of utility and cardinality.[22]

Recent theories of social choice have circumvented these problems of the classical theory by admitting partial orderings, limited agreements, non-commensurable alternatives and probabilistic judgments of choice under uncertainty, broadening the information base by even including non-utility elements, and seeking a comparative path to justice through public reasoning. Sen, in particular, has proposed the capabilities approach in which justice may be viewed in terms of opportunity rather than a specific design of how society should be organized. More substantive accounts of a just society, says Sen, may be proposed on the basis of a capabilities approach.[23]

VI

The most carefully formulated comparative theories of justice continue to rely on the method of normalization, i.e. defining norms, measuring deviations and declaring exceptions.

Despite the many technical improvements, comparative (as opposed to transcendental) theories of justice based on social choice remain firmly within the framework of normalization described earlier. Thus, there is, on the one hand, an empirically based account of actual behaviour and a comparative measure of normality as the socially prevailing average (even if this cannot be expressed as a cardinal number). On the other hand, there is a normative account, based on actual behaviour, of what is socially desirable in terms of justice. Hence, the norm-deviation and norm-exception techniques of policy remain fully relevant for these recent theories of justice.

We may exemplify this by pointing to the arguments of representative scholars, including Sen, who uphold theories of justice and welfare based on the comparative approach. Some claim that the basic insight of utilitarianism that stresses the importance of an impartial method of rational collective choice based on actual behaviour remains valid, while others emphasize the utilitarian assumption that choices must be based on good self-interested reasons and not on false or ill-informed opinion.[24] Sen himself argues that the actually prevailing normality need not coincide with the desirable norm. Thus, even when there is a strong tendency in a particular society to see people as having a single dominant identity, to make that empirical fact the normative standard would mean a denial of the norm of personal liberty.[25] Again, subjective perceptions of health are often based on popular misconceptions and prejudices and so cannot be made the normative basis for a public health policy.[26] These examples suggest that the normative standard must be based on certain universal rational principles that must prevail over the merely empirical or average normality. However, that does not mean that the normative standard is fixed through some transcendental reasoning without any reference to the heterogeneity of actual conditions. Thus, Sen says that a numerical value in terms of money or calories of the minimum needs of people to lead a reasonably healthy and dignified life cannot adequately describe the varying opportunities that may be available to people who differ in their physical ability, environmental adaptability or social status. Hence, to fix a measure of poverty based on such a numerical value of minimum resources would have no relation to the actually prevailing conditions of poverty.[27] In line with his capabilities approach, Sen also argues that the creation of opportunities need not be followed by achievement: "Freedom is not merely an instrument to achieve some end. The freedom to choose is the value, not the achievement of an end."[28] To take the example of a recent debate in India over a scheme to provide indoor toilets to millions of rural households, the argument has been made that these toilets, even when available, are not used because of social taboos on the cleaning of human waste except by specialist castes placed at the very bottom of the caste hierarchy. As a result, unclean indoor toilets, instead of contributing to public health, could in fact become a health hazard. By Sen's approach, however, the creation of the opportunity for a healthier environment is the relevant value that cannot be abandoned because the objective is not currently being achieved.

In all of these examples, what stands out is the continued relevance of the two senses of the norm – the empirically normal and the ethically normative. What follows is the continued relevance of the norm-deviation and norm-exception comparisons in the domain of policy, that is to say, in the delivery of justice. This is shown by the endorsement by many recent theorists of Adam Smith's idea of the "impartial spectator" as the position from which to properly judge questions of morality. In Sen's interpretation, the impartial spectator involves a position of open impartiality in which the spectator must actively try to see with "the eyes of other people". Hence, unlike theories that assume complete agreement on the perfectly just institution, these theories seek to achieve a degree of universality based on critical public discussion without insisting on unanimity.[29] That is the ground on which the argument could be made that although the normative standard must be based on information about actual behaviour, the former must prevail over the merely empirical normal in the determination of policy.

But although Sen does not mention it, the norm-exception form of reasoning is also wholly consistent with his comparative approach to justice. Take Smith's discussion of the varying standards of morality in societies belonging to different stages of civilization. Smith says that the qualities that are considered "either blameable or praise-worthy" vary in different ages and countries. Thus, in civilized nations, "the virtues which are founded on humanity are more cultivated", while among savages and barbarians, who are exposed to great extremes of hunger, hardship and danger, self-denial is considered the supreme virtue. Illustrating the varying standards of morality in different societies, Smith observes that infanticide was an accepted practice in many ancient societies, including Greece, where parents unable to bring up their child or forced to flee from an enemy were allowed to abandon or kill the infant. "We find, at this day, that this practice prevails among all savage nations, and in this rudest and lowest state of society it is undoubtedly more pardonable than in any other." Translated into the terms we have introduced earlier, Smith is saying that infanticide is normal in savage societies. Further, the normative standard that prevails in civilized societies must be suspended when we evaluate the norms of justice that apply to savage societies. But Smith also adds that this suspension of the desirable norm in the case of savage societies must not be allowed to persist in the form of a permissible custom in a more civilized society. Indeed, following his functionalist stage theory of civilization, Smith argues that such an abhorrent custom could not possibly endure in a civilized commercial society.[30] In short, both the norm-deviation and norm-exception techniques of comparative evaluation of justice in different societies remain relevant to Smith's impartial spectator.

Interestingly, Bentham gives exactly the same advice to his universal legislator. Discussing the strongly contrasting case of Bengal, he notes that in that country a man wanting to see the face of "a married woman from the higher class of Mahometans or Gentoos" would cause injury, but Europeans would be quite insensible to such a thing. A Brahmin might be outraged by an outcaste's touch.

> A prejudice so strong, though altogether unjust and ferocious, would require great forbearance on the part of the legislator. ... But it would be better to yield to it altogether for a time than uselessly to compromise his authority, and expose his laws to hatred.[31]

The empirical deviation is here translated into a normative exception.

To get a critical view of the comparative approach to justice based on normalization, we must make several additional specifications that will, in fact, take us beyond Sen's framework.

VII

> *The characterization of norms as universal rights such as freedom and equality is overly abstract. To be actualized as stable institutions, they must be mediated by property and fraternity (or community). Property in turn is subject to the division between capital and labour and fraternity to that between the nation-state community and the popular community. Moreover, the capital-labour property division suppresses the division between intellectual and manual labour, while community suppresses gender divisions.*

This is a somewhat schematic structural description of the modern political formation within which questions of justice are now posed. Étienne Balibar has shown that the abstract rights of freedom and equality (which, he argues, are really two opposed aspects of the same right) must be concretely institutionalized by, first, defining the rights of individual property (in the broad sense of possession of one's person and things), and second, defining the claims of the political fraternity on its members.[32] This creates the field for an unceasing tussle between freedom and equality. An emphasis on freedom results in stronger individual rights of person and property; an emphasis on equality stresses the collective demands of the community. The entire range of modern political ideologies could be said to be located within this field of actual mediations between freedom and equality.

But again, property itself constitutes a field of divisive conflict – between property as capital and property as labour. The classical theories on the subject took this division to mean the contradiction between capital and wage labour under industrial capitalism. In postcolonial countries, on the other hand, this division of the property relation is complicated not only by the continued presence of pre-capitalist forms of property and traditional subsistence production but also by the creation of state-owned enterprises and the proliferation of modern forms of non-corporate and informal enterprise. In particular, the massive proliferation in recent years of informal production and service units in Asian, African and Latin American countries, run by people dispossessed of their traditional livelihoods in agriculture and handicrafts but excluded from the labour force in the formal industrial sector, cannot be understood in terms of the classical division between property as capital and property as labour.[33]

Similarly, community too is potentially divided between that constituted by the national state and the community that claims to be constituted by the people. The two may not always coincide. This could lead to movements of separatist nationalism where a regionally concentrated population group identifying itself as a discriminated or oppressed nationality, marked by a distinct language, religion, ethnicity or other cultural-historical feature, claims to constitute a separate "people" with a self-determined right to a separate nation-state. In other cases, now increasingly common in postcolonial countries, a populist movement, usually under a charismatic leader, claims to voice the demands of "the people" against the constituted state authority of the status quo represented by the established national parties or bureaucracy which are designated as enemies of the people. The antagonistic politics of populism sees itself as an insurrection of the authentic community of the people against those who claim to formally represent the national community.

There are other lines of division that are suppressed by the mediations described above. Thus, the capital-labour division of property suppresses the hierarchical division in all modern economies between intellectual and manual labour. In particular, the recent proliferation of the service economy, including banking and financial services, has thoroughly displaced the primacy of industrial manufacturing in advanced capitalist economies. So has the emphasis on "human capital" based on higher education as the preferred source of gainful employment. On the other hand, in a country like India, the modern division between manual and intellectual labour has allowed the rearticulation of the traditional religion-based hierarchy of caste into a secular hierarchy, supposedly premised on individual merit and ability but largely mirroring the old caste divisions. Finally, the collective claims of the community on its members suppress the gender division by assuming the heterosexual male as the normalized citizen with equal rights; women belong to the political fraternity only as subsidiary members.

VIII

> *On the international plane, collective justice requires an acknowledgement of the historical fact that there are oppressor and oppressed nations. Hence, there must be recognition of the right of self-determination of nations and peoples and the formal equality of all sovereign states. Within nations, justice requires the recognition of the collective rights of minorities and oppressed groups.*

We may now specify some relevant issues of justice in postcolonial countries. The question of collective justice is one that is virtually impossible to pose within the framework of social choice theory since the foundational assumption of that theory is of an individual agent exercising choice. Even within the broader field of rights-based liberal theory, the idea of collective rights does not enjoy wide acceptance. The only collective right generally recognized is that of the sovereignty of nation-states grounded in some sort of legitimate popular consent. But this right of self-determination of nations was not recognized as a universal principle until the middle of the twentieth century, after a century of anti-imperialist and democratic struggles around the world. These struggles succeeded in posing the historical question of justice in relations between oppressor and oppressed nations. The end of colonial empires in the middle of the twentieth century universalized the nation-state form as the normal form of the modern state.

But even though the principle of formal equality of state sovereignty is recognized in the General Assembly of the United Nations where each member-state has a single vote, it is flouted in the Security Council where the five permanent members have veto power. There are numerous instances in contemporary international political, economic, military and legal relations where, despite the formal equality of sovereignty, some states are able to exercise the privilege of treating other states as less than equally sovereign. To invoke the comparative framework explained earlier, formal equality of sovereignty establishes a common standard by which deviations from normal state-ness can be measured across the world in terms of economic, political, military or cultural criteria. Some powerful states then claim the privilege of suspending the norm of equal sovereignty in order to justify policies of intervention seeking to punish, reform or educate deviant states. The question of collective justice from the postcolonial point of view is: should some states be allowed to exercise the imperial privilege of suspending the norm of equal sovereignty or should there be a more democratic global procedure involving all nation-states for intervening when necessary in the sovereign jurisdiction of a state?[34]

There are other issues of collective justice involving the historical record of imperialism that have been raised in recent years. For instance, certain instances in imperial history are seen as extraordinarily atrocious and outrageous for which apologies and even compensation have been demanded from former imperial powers. Writing at the time of decolonization, Frantz Fanon had demanded that the imperial powers be asked to pay reparations for the damage and plunder they had committed in the colonies. "Colonialism and imperialism" he said,

> have not paid their score when they withdraw their flags and their police forces from our territories. ... [Reparations] should be the ratification of a double realization: the realization by the colonized people that *it is their due*, and the realization by the capitalist powers that in fact *they must pay*.[35]

Though no general claim of reparation has been made by any postcolonial country, specific claims continue to be made, say, for the return of antiquities and other items of national heritage currently in the possession of Western museums and repositories.

Moving to the plane of domestic national politics, the matter of community rights is not fully resolved by the formal recognition of nation-state sovereignty. The question remains of who legitimately represents the collective entity of the national community and whether minority communities are properly a part of the popular sovereignty on which the legitimacy of the nation-state is supposedly founded. One set of issues here of collective justice concerns the historical consequences of conquest and settler colonialism in the Americas, Australia, New Zealand and parts of southern Africa. The indigenous peoples of the Americas, Australia and New Zealand have been reduced to marginal and discriminated minorities with virtually no participation in the national community. The call of justice there has been to seek redress for the historical wrongs committed on the indigenous peoples and protection of their distinct social and cultural identities. In the settler colonies of Africa, on the other hand, the end of colonial empire led to the assertion of popular sovereignty by the black majority, while white settlers were reduced to wealthy and propertied minorities. Postcolonial justice there has taken the form of a debate about whether white settlers should be expropriated and their lands redistributed to the black majority or included within a new national formation as equal citizens. The question of settler colonialism has assumed yet another form, even after the age of colonial empires, in the continued Israeli occupation and settlement of Palestinian lands. The international and national planes have overlapped there in posing the question of collective justice.

But there are several other forms in which issues of collective justice manifest themselves in domestic national politics. Some of these concern claims of groups that represent majorities in particular regions of a country. These claims to justice could be met by the devolution of certain sovereign powers to regional or local authorities, as in a federation. Thus, collective justice is achieved through a territorial redistribution of the sovereignty of the nation-state. But there could be demands for collective justice from groups that are not territorially concentrated. Such demands made by religious, linguistic or ethnic minorities, for instance, may be met by making exceptional provisions to the norm of equal citizenship. Thus, in India, the rights of religious minorities and scheduled castes and tribes are protected by enacting exceptions to the fundamental right of equality before the law. It should be noted that the argument (made by Sen, for instance) that collective identity claims violate personal liberty ignores the actuality of those claims voiced through democratic mobilization. Addressing such demands for collective justice within a framework of rational legal procedures is one of the key challenges faced by postcolonial countries. I will have more to say on this point later.

IX

The social heterogeneity that exists in most postcolonial countries creates demands for justice quite different from those experienced in Western democracies. The governance of the informal sector, electoral populism, the demand for arbitrary power to promote the good, and differentiated citizenship to accommodate religious or ethnic difference are some examples. Justice is sought to be delivered by making exceptions to the legal norm.

The social space of citizenship over which legal-constitutional norms are supposed to apply equally and uniformly achieved a large degree of homogeneity in the countries of Western Europe and North America by the early twentieth century. First established as the institutional principles of bourgeois society, these norms were gradually extended to include the rest of society through the extension of the suffrage to workers and women, the universalization of primary and secondary education, the spread of civil-social associations including national trade unions among the working classes and the creation of national political parties with mass electoral following. Before the coming of new immigrants from non-European countries in the 1960s, therefore, Western capitalist democracies held a broadly homogeneous view of citizenship. As a result, transcendental theories of justice that assumed the necessary fiction of complete social agreement as the foundational constitutional moment did have a certain plausibility. Even John Rawls's theory of overlapping consensus as the necessary basis of political decisions could be seen as a feasible foundation for justice.[36] Theories of justice, such as Sen's, that begin by distancing themselves from the requirement of complete agreement are propelled mainly by the awareness that the problems encountered in postcolonial countries like India cannot be addressed except by acknowledging their enormous social heterogeneity.

A key feature of the political economy of many postcolonial countries today, including that of China, is the proliferation of the so-called informal economy. This is the result of the process of primitive accumulation of capital by which direct producers such as peasants and traditional craftspeople lose their means of production. But given the capital-intensive nature of contemporary manufacturing industries (a requirement imposed by global conditions of technology), most of the dispossessed masses cannot be absorbed in the formally constituted growth sectors of the economy. It must be remembered that the accepted techniques that were available to European countries in the nineteenth and early twentieth centuries for the political management of primitive accumulation – massive emigration to the Americas and the Antipodes, and millions of deaths in wars, epidemics and famines – are no longer available to postcolonial regimes. Hence, the proliferating informal economy which competes in the same marketplace with corporate capital has to survive partly by self-exploitation (most informal units are operated by family labour) and partly by the violation of laws that regulate trade licences, taxation, labour, pollution, civic amenities, etc. in the formal sector. Those who work in informal units make demands on government to treat their cases as deserving exceptional treatment. Government often responds to these politically articulated demands by making temporary and contingent exceptions. The result is a massive piling up of exceptions to the law in order to meet the demands of justice.[37]

The question is thus raised: is justice better served by non-arbitrary procedures of the equal application of the law, or the contextual and possibly arbitrary judgment that addresses the peculiarities of a particular case? This question cannot be answered in the context of postcolonial societies in the same way that, for instance, Rawls answers it for liberal-democratic Western society – by insisting on the priority of fair procedures over substantively good outcomes.[38] The reason is that unlike most Western democracies, the foundational moment of constitution-making in postcolonial countries was not an attempt to stabilize the results of a revolution that had been completed. On the contrary, the constitution often became the legal machinery to enable a social transformation that was still to come. Hence, the fundamental laws were not necessarily seen as a set of prior commitments that would place binding constraints on legislative or executive action in future. Rather, they were often specified such that they would not stand in the way of discretionary or even arbitrary decisions by the government to bring about substantively just outcomes.[39] Thus, for instance, the right to property was not included in the list of fundamental rights in the Indian constitution because doing so might have come in the way of ending landlordism and undertaking agrarian reform. Similarly, specific exceptions were made to the right to equality before the law in order to protect the personal laws and educational and cultural institutions of religious minorities and reserve positions in legislative bodies, government employment and educational institutions for persons from the scheduled castes and tribes. Initially seen as a temporary measure, these lists have not only become permanent features of Indian life but have expanded to include exceptional provisions for "other backward classes" and become internally differentiated by degrees of backwardness.

The tussle between legal-constitutional norms and discretionary power to declare exceptions continues in many postcolonial countries. The problem is compounded by electoral mobilizations based on populist demands. These movements, usually led by charismatic figures, demand specific acts of justice (whether symbolic or substantive is often not at issue) for the "real people" who they claim have not been represented before in the corridors of power. Many such demands are met by elected governments not by redefining normative constitutional provisions but by making the case for exceptional treatment of specific demands by specific groups. This feeds into the vast apparatus of governmentality that has proliferated in all postcolonial countries as administrative techniques for taking care of population groups not on the basis of the ethical claims of citizenship but empirically established needs of subsistence, habitation, education, health, etc. Populist politics strengthens the force of arbitrary legislative or executive power to deliver substantive justice.

There is a corresponding criticism of the methods of procedural justice as well. It is widely alleged in India that judicial procedures, apparently aimed at fairness, are opaque, alienating and inordinately time-consuming. The wealthy and well-connected are much better able to use the judicial machinery to their advantage than those from the poorer sections of society. There is a strong popular opinion, reflecting traditional notions, that a fair, personally upright and impartial judge is far more likely to deliver justice than an impersonal system of procedures.[40] Curiously, this criticism appears to be shared by the higher echelons of the Indian judiciary itself which introduced in the 1980s the unique institution of the Public Interest Litigation under which anyone may bring any matter of public interest to the attention of the court, without regard for the usual requirements of *locus standi*. The court may, in such cases, disregard the adversarial system, have a case argued by a friend of the court, call in experts, set up independent inquiries under its own supervision and issue orders to branches of government. The court may even start proceedings on its own initiative. As a result, the judiciary in India has acquired a range of legislative and even executive powers unprecedented in any liberal constitutional system in the world, all in the interest of delivering substantive justice.

I am tempted to remark here that some of these consequences of fundamental social heterogeneity have recently appeared in Europe and North America with the arrival there of large numbers of non-European migrants. The dilemma is being posed in those countries: can the full extension of equal citizenship to these recent entrants, many of whom live and work there without proper legal entitlement, meet the demands of social heterogeneity, or should they be governed as exceptions, thus in effect producing a form of differentiated citizenship? Ironically, it would seem, the postcolonial condition has crept into the body politic of even the erstwhile imperial countries. Looking to another part of the world, a form of differentiated citizenship is effectively the predominant framework of governance in the countries of the Persian Gulf region where most inhabitants are not citizens.

X

An adequate postcolonial theory of justice must combine procedural fairness with substantively just outcomes.

The political form of making heterogeneous demands for justice in postcolonial societies is double-edged. On the one hand, mobilizations voicing demands of specific groups have proliferated and intensified, leading to the creation of a mountain of exceptions for virtually every provision of the law. On the other hand, equal treatment and fair procedures under the law have been compromised. It is undeniable that frequent resort to arbitrary power results in uncertainty about the uniform application of the law, resort to illegal and often violent mobilizations to press for arbitrary action, decisions taken by one government being reversed by the next and an inherent tendency toward authoritarian executive power. The two opposed forces are immanent in claims to justice in postcolonial countries.

It is interesting to note that the extraordinary powers acquired by the Indian judiciary in recent times have been justified on two entirely opposed grounds. On the one hand, the courts have acted to defend basic constitutional norms against arbitrary laws passed by legislatures and arbitrary decisions of the executive. On the other hand, courts have sometimes bypassed established procedure to directly deliver justice to "the people" because, they allege, corrupt or inefficient government functionaries have failed to do what the law requires them to do. The dilemma of postcolonial justice is visible in the two opposed justifications for judicial activism.

XI

The institutions of postcolonial democracy provide greater opportunity for procedural fairness while authoritarian institutions may sometimes produce substantively just outcomes.

While populist electoral politics is often blamed for arbitrary, unproductive and wasteful decisions in the name of delivering social justice, it is arguable that electoral democracy actually provides greater opportunity not only for hitherto marginal groups to voice their demands but, surprisingly, also for procedural fairness. This is not immediately obvious. Apparently, postcolonial democracies, such as India's, seem to be marked by an endless string of populist promises by competing political parties which are often met by the exercise of arbitrary and sometimes unlawful discretionary power causing severe strains between different branches of government (between the political leadership and the permanent bureaucracy, for instance, or between the judiciary and the executive) and unmanageable crises in government finances. The horizon of policy-making tends to shrink to the period up to the next election, while the beneficiaries tend to be partisan constituencies. Decisions that could yield durable social results with a wider social base in the longer term tend to be ignored since they do not bring immediate electoral returns. Even when the justification for populist decisions is the achievement of specific demands for justice relating to the material conditions of living of the poor and marginal sections of society, the effect is merely an illusion since no stable foundations are being laid for those just outcomes to become sustainable.

This has produced a critique of electoral democracy as a process that impedes long-term investment and development strategies in postcolonial countries characterized by mass poverty and social backwardness. The counter-argument is then offered: restrict the space for electoral representation and instead create institutions of decision-making where experts, planners, investors and others holding long-term stakes in social justice can come together to make authoritative choices that would transform the economy and society of postcolonial countries. Recall that when the comparative approach to justice was launched by utilitarians in the nineteenth century, while representative government was declared the universally valid normative standard, the universally valid exception was enlightened despotism. The same argument based on the norm-deviation and norm-exception structure continues to be made today. Note, for instance, the justifications that have been offered in recent years for ousting popularly elected governments in Egypt and Thailand. Electoral democracy, the allegation goes, is inefficient, partisan, corrupt, slow and indecisive. It is unsuitable for postcolonial countries where the need of the hour is rapid economic growth and social transformation.

The fact is, however, that the conditions that produce populist demands are not restricted to the process of electoral democracy alone; they are germane to the social heterogeneity that is the historical inheritance of the postcolonial condition itself. In other words, even authoritarian regimes cannot avoid the pressure to satisfy at least some populist demands in order to create an acceptable condition of legitimacy for their rule. And they are liable to be equally, if not more, arbitrary in making those populist decisions. However, being authoritarian, they will not be subject to the constant scrutiny of a public and the periodic approval of an electorate. Hence, rather counter-intuitively, it turns out that while authoritarian regimes might well achieve some substantively just outcomes through their arbitrary actions, there is greater likelihood in an electoral democracy for procedural fairness to be upheld.

Speaking of the comparative approach to justice, it is worth remembering that the orthodox view in the utilitarian tradition is to compare policy alternatives in terms of their consequences. Recent theorists like Sen have sought to discount the consequentialist approach and emphasize the value of capabilities in terms of the opportunities that are created for individual choice. Nevertheless, the comparison of consequences in measurable statistical terms has become deeply ingrained in contemporary social discourse: it is part of the prevalent common sense of policy experts, journalists and politicians. As a result, the desire for some form of enlightened despotism as the more suitable means to achieve social justice in the less developed countries feeds on the record of the achievements of many authoritarian regimes of Asia in ending poverty, illiteracy, undernourishment, extreme gender inequality, etc. Unlike the advanced capitalist countries of the West, authoritarianism has a strong social constituency in the postcolonial world where rapid social transformation is on the agenda.

Hence, a commitment to democracy as the legitimate framework for securing justice cannot be taken for granted in postcolonial countries. It has to be fought for in the battlefield of politics. A theory of justice, no matter how philosophically robust, can never be adequate in meeting the requirements of political mobilization, leadership, persuasion and astute judgment. The latter belong to the domain of the art of politics; no philosophical theory can expound their principles.

Notes

1 This chapter was first written for the workshop "Is There an Adequate Theory of Justice?" held in March 2015 at the Indian Institute of Advanced Study in Shimla. I am grateful to Sobhanlal Datta Gupta, Gopal Guru, Maidul Islam, Gurpreet Mahajan, Sundar Sarukkai and other participants for their comments. I have also benefited greatly from discussions on the paper with Akeel Bilgrami.
2 Karl Marx, "Critique of the Gotha Programme" (1875), in Karl Marx and Frederick Engels, *Collected Works*, vol. 24 (Moscow: Progress Publishers, 1968), pp. 81–99.
3 "Enlightened Anarchy: A Political Ideal", in *The Collected Works of Mahatma Gandhi [CWMG]* (New Delhi: Publications Division, 1958–), vol. 68, p. 265.
4 For example, CWMG, vol. 35, pp. 489–90; CWMG, vol. 45, pp. 328–9.
5 For example, CWMG, vol. 59, pp. 61–7; CWMG, vol. 50, pp. 226–7.
6 Thus, for example, Speech at AICC Meeting, Wardha, 15 January 1942, CWMG, vol. 75, p. 220; Letter to Labhshankar Mehta, 14 April 1926, CWMG, vol. 30, p. 283.
7 Amartya Sen, *The Idea of Justice* (London: Allen Lane, 2009). I am ignoring Sen's characterization of theories of perfect institutions as akin to *nīti* and those of substantively just outcomes as *nyāya* since the distinction is apt to be misleading. *Nīti* in the Indian scholarly tradition is associated with the *śāstra* of *rājanīti* of which the various *arthaśāstra* texts are the most well known. If compared with the European disciplines, these would come closest to the *raison d'État*

literature of the sixteenth to the eighteenth century in which the survival and well-being of the state and its ruler was the primary interest. *Nyāya*, on the other hand, is principally associated with the philosophical discipline of logic.

8 Sen, *Idea*, pp. 66–72.

9 John Locke, "*Second Treatise, §49*", in *Two Treatises on Government*, ed. Peter Laslett (Cambridge: Cambridge University Press, 1988), p. 301.

10 Jeremy Bentham, *An Introduction to the Principles of Morals and Legislation* (1789; Oxford: Clarendon Press, 1907), ch. xvii, § 2.

11 Bentham, "Essay on the Influence of Time and Place in Matters of Legislation", in *The Works of Jeremy Bentham*, ed. John Bowring, vol. 1 (Edinburgh: William Tait, 1843), p. 171. I am immensely grateful to Philip Schofield, director of the Bentham Project at University College London, for generously giving me access to the revised version of this essay which is to appear in a volume of Bentham's *Collected Works*. I have accordingly amended where necessary the text of the essay that appears in the 1843 collection. Schofield has also confirmed that the essay was written by Bentham in 1780-82 and was intended to form a part of the *Principles of Morals and Legislation*.

12 "Influence of Time and Place", p. 172.

13 Ibid.

14 Ibid, p. 177.

15 Ibid, p. 173.

16 Ian Hacking, *The Taming of Chance* (Cambridge: Cambridge University Press, 1990), pp. 160–9.

17 Leonard Krieger, *An Essay on the Theory of Enlightened Despotism* (Chicago: University of Chicago Press, 1975), p. 39.

18 Uday Singh Mehta, *Liberalism and Empire: A Study in Nineteenth-century British Liberal Thought* (Chicago: University of Chicago Press, 1999).

19 John Stuart Mill, *Considerations on Representative Government* (1861; Cambridge: Cambridge University Press, 2010), ch. xviii.

20 Especially Michel Foucault, *Discipline and Punish: The Birth of the Prison*, tr. Alan Sheridan (Harmondsworth: Penguin, 1977).

21 Hacking, *Taming of Chance*.

22 For detailed discussion of the problems of classical utilitarian theory and ways to get around them, see Amartya Sen and Bernard Williams, eds., *Utilitarianism and Beyond* (Cambridge: Cambridge University Press, 1982).

23 Sen, *Idea of Justice*, p. 232.

24 See the essays by John C. Harsanyi, "Morality and the Theory of Rational Behaviour", and J. A. Mirrlees, "The Economic Uses of Utilitarianism", in *Utilitarianism and Beyond*, eds. Sen and Williams (Cambridge: Cambridge University Press, 1982), pp. 39–62 and 63–84.

25 Sen, *Idea of Justice*, p. 247.

26 Ibid, p. 285.

27 Ibid, p. 255,

28 Ibid, p. 237.

29 Ibid, pp. 130–8.

30 All of these citations are from Adam Smith, *The Theory of Moral Sentiments* (London: A. Millar, 1761), Part V, chapter II.

31 Bentham, "Influence of Time and Place", p. 181.

32 Étienne Balibar, *Masses, Classes, Ideas: Studies on Politics and Philosophy before and after Marx*, tr. James Swenson (New York: Routledge, 1993), pp. 39–60; Balibar, *Equaliberty: Political Essays*, tr. James Ingram (Durham: Duke University Press, 2014).

33 The point has been conceptually formulated in a radically new way in Kalyan Sanyal, *Rethinking Capitalist Development: Primitive Accumulation,*

Governmentality and Post-colonial Capitalism (London and New Delhi: Routledge, 2007).

34 I have discussed this point at greater length in Partha Chatterjee, *The Black Hole of Empire: History of a Global Practice of Power* (Princeton: Princeton University Press, 2012), chapter 10.

35 Frantz Fanon, *The Wretched of the Earth*, tr. Constance Farrington (1962; Harmondsworth: Penguin, 1967), pp. 101–3.

36 John Rawls, *Political Liberalism* (New York: Columbia University Press, 1993), especially pp. 133–72.

37 I have discussed this at greater length in Chatterjee, *The Politics of the Governed: Reflections on Politics in Most of the World* (New York: Columbia University Press, 2004) and *Lineages of Political Society: Studies in Postcolonial Democracy* (Ranikhet: Permanent Black; New York: Columbia University Press, 2011).

38 Rawls, *Political Liberalism*, pp. 174–211.

39 See Partha Chatterjee, "Introduction: Postcolonial Legalism", *Comparative Studies of South Asia, Africa and the Middle East*, 34 (2014), 2, pp. 224–7. See, in particular, the essays by Sandipto Dasgupta, Thushara Hewage, Rohit De and Anuj Bhuwania in the same issue.

40 During the anti-corruption campaign in India led by Anna Hazare in 2011, it was suggested that an ombudsman institution of the Lokpal be created consisting of persons of unimpeachable moral integrity who would have powers to conduct investigations into allegations of official corruption and pass summary judgments.

List of works cited

Étienne Balibar, *Masses, Classes, Ideas: Studies on Politics and Philosophy before and after Marx*, tr. James Swenson (New York: Routledge, 1993)

_____, *Equaliberty: Political Essays*, tr. James Ingram (Durham, NC: Duke University Press, 2014)

Jeremy Bentham, *The Works of Jeremy Bentham*, vol. 1, ed. John Bowring (Edinburgh: William Tait, 1843)

———, *An Introduction to the Principles of Morals and Legislation* (1789; Oxford: Clarendon Press, 1907)

Partha Chatterjee, *The Politics of the Governed: Reflections on Politics in Most of the World* (New York: Columbia University Press, 2004)

———, *Lineages of Political Society: Studies in Postcolonial Democracy* (Ranikhet: Permanent Black; New York: Columbia University Press, 2011)

_____, *The Black Hole of Empire: History of a Global Practice of Power* (Princeton: Princeton University Press, 2012)

———, ed. "Symposium on Postcolonial Legalism", *Comparative Studies of South Asia, Africa and the Middle East*, 34 (2014), 2, pp. 224–267.

Frantz Fanon, *The Wretched of the Earth*, tr. Constance Farrington (1962; Harmondsworth: Penguin, 1967)

Michel Foucault, *Discipline and Punish: The Birth of the Prison*, tr. Alan Sheridan (Harmondsworth: Penguin, 1977)

M. K. Gandhi, *The Collected Works of Mahatma Gandhi* [CWMG] (New Delhi: Publications Division, 1958–)

Ian Hacking, *The Taming of Chance* (Cambridge: Cambridge University Press, 1990)

Leonard Krieger, *An Essay on the Theory of Enlightened Despotism* (Chicago: University of Chicago Press, 1975)

John Locke, *Two Treatises on Government*, ed. Peter Laslett (Cambridge: Cambridge University Press, 1988)

Karl Marx, "Critique of the Gotha Programme", (1875) in Karl Marx and Frederick Engels, *Collected Works*, vol. 24 (Moscow: Progress Publishers, 1968).

John Rawls, *Political Liberalism* (New York: Columbia University Press, 1993)

Kalyan Sanyal, *Rethinking Capitalist Development: Primitive Accumulation, Governmentality and Post-colonial Capitalism* (London and New Delhi: Routledge, 2007)

Amartya Sen, *The Idea of Justice* (London: Allen Lane, 2009)

Amartya Sen and Bernard Williams, eds., *Utilitarianism and Beyond* (Cambridge: Cambridge University Press, 1982)

Uday Singh Mehta, *Liberalism and Empire: A Study in Nineteenth-century British Liberal Thought* (Chicago: University of Chicago Press, 1999)

Adam Smith, *The Theory of Moral Sentiments* (London: A. Millar, 1761)

John Stuart Mill, *Considerations on Representative Government* (1861; Cambridge: Cambridge University Press, 2010)

7 Extending the sphere of justice

The dilemmas of everyday life

Gurpreet Mahajan

On June 16 and 17, 2013, heavy rainfall and cloud bursts led to flash floods and landslides in the state of Uttarakhand. Several settlements and villages were washed away and as bridges broke and roads caved in, almost 75,000 people, including pilgrims and tourists, were trapped in the Kedarnath Valley and other parts of the state. At the Temple of Kedarnath itself about 7000–8000 persons were stranded; as the Temple and the area around it came under water, many pilgrims lost their lives. The panic that set in, and the stampede that followed, yielded some more casualties. Since the main highway and the connecting roads were damaged, it was difficult to reach the survivors of this calamity. The only possible way of rescuing the pilgrims at Kedarnath was to airlift them. However, the place had only one landing site. So even when the government decided to deploy helicopters, it was evident that the aircraft would not be able to make more than one or two flights that day. In other words, seats were limited and everyone could not be evacuated all at once. In principle everyone was to be evacuated and brought to a secure and safe place, but in actual practice only a few people would be rescued at one time or even one day.

Under the circumstances what was the right thing to do? What was a fair and just way of dealing with those affected by this situation? Who should be rescued first? What criterion should be applied for this? These were the urgent questions. This is not of course the first time that such questions, involving issues of justice, had arisen. In 2010, Ladakh and the region of Leh witnessed flash floods and a major landslide. Similar questions presented themselves even there; and, before that, in the rescue operations during the 2004 Tsunami that was centered in the Indian Ocean. When natural disasters of this scale occur, the discussion invariably is about techniques of disaster management: the institutional preparedness, the need for coordination, rescue work, relief operations, and coordination between agencies become the focus of attention. The major question of justice that every disaster presents is rarely debated or considered with any seriousness. Even when the discussion on the distribution of relief fund occurs, and caste and community emerge as relevant categories, sociological analyses take over.

DOI: 10.4324/9780429355974-7

Political theorists and philosophers move into the background; they rarely intervene and discuss the question of justice that is posed in these situations.

The chapter basically addresses this neglect. It argues that most theories of justice offer a principle for the just organization of society rather than guidance about just action; particularly what a just action would require in a specific situation. To a considerable extent this is on account of the presumed dichotomy between theory and practice, principle and policy. Theorists tend to assert the primacy of the former and focus on identifying a principle or a norm that is constitutive of justice; all else is seen as a matter of application or policy, almost as if the latter entails mainly an easy, unproblematic and logical extension of the principle. This dichotomized mode of thinking is however a problem, and it limits available theories of justice rendering them inadequate and unsatisfactory. An adequate theory of justice must begin from a contrary point of view: that is, by bridging the hiatus between principle and policy. Instead of leaving policy to technocrats it must recognize that the practice might make our theory and the proposed principle of justice indefensible, or even unjustified. While building a theory of justice one must reflect on concrete situations in which questions of fairness and justice are asked and see if we have satisfactory ways of responding to the challenges that we confront in everyday life.

Unfortunately the common practice is to point the finger at decision-makers and say that politics intervened; hence, the principle was sacrificed and it caused the ensuing injustice. In some cases this does indeed happen; we find personal or individual considerations taking over the space for reasoned argumentation. But that is only a small fragment of the problem. The more serious challenge emerges when the dilemmas posed by institutional practices and those confronted in concrete contexts are simply set aside and ignored. Or else, when decision-makers rely on accepted ways of thinking: that is, they invoke, what Walzer refers to as, settled and shared ways of dealing with or distributing burdens and rewards (Walzer 1983). As political theorists we are obligated to examine how communities and decision-makers respond in specific situations and explicate why certain responses appear inadequate or even blatantly unjust. Political theorists need to intervene in the everyday matters of politics and attempt to contribute to the making of a public reason that is self-reflective and has the capacity to guide us in other contexts.

*

Questions of justice confront us routinely in everyday life; yet, the dilemmas that we face remain rather peripheral in the discussions on justice. Contemporary theorists of justice, such as Rawls, Dworkin, Nozick, and Walzer, concentrate on principles which should determine the basic structure of society. Analysts further examine these identified principles; at times they debate methodological issues surrounding them and ask whether the universalist claim is at all tenable? Whether we have a single principle which can be applied in different contexts involving justice? Or, as Walzer argues, the principle of justice may vary from one context to another: for example, what is just when recruiting for university jobs may not appear just when we are considering healthcare for citizens (Walzer 1983; also see, Miller 1999). Do we then have many principles of justice and what is adequate varies from one sphere of activity to another? Debates of this nature continue to preoccupy theorists everywhere. The striking element is that despite the differences between the universalists and the contextualists neither of them question the need to identify some principle(s) that should guide our understanding of what is just. The only thing that separates them is that for the pluralists the given principle is relevant in some contexts and not all, while most others are searching for a principle that can serve us well in all spheres of modern life.

This singular emphasis on identifying a principle (something that has for long been central to normative political theory) has engendered a dichotomy between theory and policy. The underlying assumption in this framework is that the task of theory is to find a principle that defines what is just while policy addresses questions of application. For instance, if the principle is that inequalities in societies must be arranged so as to work to the advantage of the worst-off (Rawls's second principle 1971:302) political theorists provide justifications for this principle; some criticize this principle and suggest alternative ways of discussing what constitutes a just distribution. But all of them assume that such matters as identifying who is the least advantaged, what resources should be redistributed to them, or how should the identified social goods be distributed to the targeted group are all matters of policy. The consequence of this way of thinking is that theorists debate the adequacy of a principle and so-called policy analysts focus on the latter. Theorists dismiss the latter set of issues as questions of application and policy buffs tend increasingly to believe that these questions can be settled empirically and scientifically. Taking a cue from Max Weber, they undertake a cost-benefit analysis of the options available through a discussion of what is the most efficient way of accomplishing a given goal.

The end result of this dichotomized understanding is that theory becomes the realm of argumentation and policy is taken over by those who are identified as experts. Neither makes space for the political: this, in a way, is a new form of "scientisation" (a term used by the Frankfurt School to refer to the limits of enlightenment rationalism) that has occurred in recent times where conflict and contests over what is the desired principle are somewhat sanitized. Invariably, this has helped to camouflage the structures of power and ideology that are always present in the public sphere.

We need therefore to question this mode of dichotomized thinking about the social and political world. Questions of justice are not, and should not be, reduced primarily to the discovery of a principle. One must also ask how justice is at work through different institutions and in different contexts. After all a society is known by the manner in which its individual members and institutions function; even more importantly, one cannot assume that once the basic structure of society is settled, matters of justice have been adequately addressed. For the basic structure may be based on a just principle, but the everyday practices may not be so. At times, the apparent injustices of the latter may prompt people to question the just-ness of the basic structure itself. One has only to look at the issue of reservations in India to appreciate the need to overcome the divide between theory and practice. There is still a consensus (a few dissenting voices notwithstanding) on the need to have some policies of affirmative action; there is also an indirect endorsement of the Rawlsian principle that inequalities can be accepted if they are of benefit to the least advantaged members of society. Yet, the modes of identifying beneficiaries (excluding some vulnerable groups and including other more politically powerful groups) as well as deciding in which sphere inequalities should be permitted, in what form, and to what extent are matters that have thrown up doubts not only about the policy formulated but also about the principle involved. This is not entirely surprising as a just order requires not only a principle but also a just ordering of institutions and just dispensations.

The principle underlying affirmative action reminds us that equality cannot always be pursued by treating everybody alike in all respects but determining which differences should count and be considered relevant is also important for pursuing justice. Should differences of circumstance – such as income, location, family situation – matter or should we focus on historically existing forms of discrimination – for instance, those based on race and caste; or should we focus on those who are politically marginalized in the current scenario? Dispensation of justice requires that we go beyond the mere identification of principle and consider how we should deal with each of these dimensions and act in a given context. By itself the principle offers little help or direction in dealing with the dilemmas that we confront in determinate situations. In fact the contradictions that concrete practices throw up point both to the incompleteness and the inadequacy of a given principle – even one that appears to be appropriate at the general and more abstract level.

What is also important is to recognize that justice requires, at least most of the time, striking a balance between two principles, and often between two values. In the case of reservations one has to balance the concern for keeping posts open with ensuring a level playing field; both principles are important for justice. When either is sacrificed, then justice does not appear to be done. We confront a similar need to balance different principles in the distribution of other social goods. Take, for instance, the case of healthcare: one has to balance the principle of treating everyone alike with urgency of need. On the one hand, a hospital must treat all the patients alike when it comes to admitting them or preparing a schedule of surgeries in the available operation theater; on the other, it must also make space for accommodating accident victims whose need for medical attention and surgical intervention is extremely urgent. If we adhere to any one principle all the time, then justice may well be sacrificed on many occasions. If an accident victim is not accommodated and this diminishes the chances of her survival while pre-scheduled surgeries are performed, then most persons will agree that injustice was done. At the same time if patients already admitted in the hospital are waiting endlessly for their medical treatment/surgery, then too justice would be sacrificed. In other words, the hospital has to find a way of balancing these two different concerns. While everyone's needs must be attended to in a way that gives equal consideration to each person, it is also necessary to prioritize the case of those whose medical need appears more urgent.

Striking the right balance is never easy or simple and it is difficult to provide a manual for it. But we can take concrete instances where it seems (to us or at least to large numbers of people) that justice was not done, and initiate a discussion on which principles should matter and what might be the right balance between contending principles. Only then are we likely to move in the direction of creating a just system. If, to continue with the same example, the hospital was to assess urgent needs in terms of who is willing to pay more or who is connected to the social and political elite, one could begin by asking whether this is a reasonable and defensible way of distributing this particular social good. Michael Walzer is right in suggesting that the nature of the social good is important for determining what is just, and in this case one might ask whether possessing wealth or position is essential or intrinsic to the distribution of health care. Arriving at the principles appropriate for distribution of a particular social good and finding a desirable balance between these principles requires a public discussion. It cannot be known or determined in advance. We need to activate forums of public debate and discussion for the sake of arriving at a consensus; even if that ideal situation is never reached, public debate is necessary to understand which principles need to be accommodated and which practices violate these principles.

For this reason one can at best speak of what are the requirements of an adequate theory of justice but never offer a theory of justice that can claim to be complete, comprehensive, and adequate. Different theories of justice might alert us to conditions and elements that an adequate theory of justice must take seriously, and give some suggestions about what justice might entail. But that is all that they can be expected to do. Therefore, one has to reorient oneself and reconsider what we are looking for in an adequate theory of justice.

*

There is another challenge that theorization on justice confronts, but we rarely consider it seriously – namely, what justice entails in situations that are uncommon or extraordinary. Since theories of justice, from Rawls to Nozick, Walzer to Miller, focus on what is a just ordering of society or a just distribution of the desired social goods, they focus on the overarching structure of society. They tend to speak of distributions in normal situations, overlooking all those events and occurrences that are characterized as uncommon or extraordinary. In actuality the so-called extraordinary events are not that uncommon and there are far too many situations in the life of the society where the ordinarily accepted principles and patterns of distribution need to be assessed, reformulated, or reconfigured. The flash floods in Uttarakhand, with which this chapter began, is a case in point. At the face of it what happened in Uttarakhand appears to be a one-off thing, which requires short-term adjustment or temporary deviation from the established norm. In reality the Uttarakhand floods of 2013 may have been unprecedented in scale for this region, but extraordinary situations of this kind are not uncommon. Every year there are floods in some part of India and at times in the same part of a given state. When we focus on the just ordering of society one can readily label such situations as exceptional and focus on creating a society where the hardships associated with displacement and sudden evacuation are extremely rare, if not entirely absent. But even as we work towards that ideal just ordering one must find ways of dealing with such extraordinary situations in ways that appear fair and reasonable. Being just cannot be simply deferred and put on hold in the interim period.

It is from this perspective that I return to the case of Uttarakhand floods. I might also add here that cases of this kind are important for another reason. Rawls begins his theory of justice with the cautionary note that we can only apply his framework under conditions of moderate scarcity. In other words, in situations of acute scarcity the principles suggested by him are likely to flounder. The flash floods in Uttarakhand created a condition of acute vulnerability; in such a context, where accepted principles are unlikely to work, one would expect the community's self-understanding to kick in. Even if we disagree with Walzer that a conception of justice that has ordered the life of the community over a long period of time would be the most appropriate one, one would imagine that such a deeply embedded and shared understanding would be a resource that people will fall back upon in at least extraordinary situations. Looking at some of the responses that came from the government and the people it would be interesting to see if this does indeed happen. What principles were invoked for dealing with such a situation and how adequate were they? The next few pages take up these questions. Among other things they show that even in exceptional situations, like that of Uttarakhand floods, different principles are invoked and it is exceedingly difficult to settle the differences in perspective in advance. At the end of the day, one needs an active public sphere which engages critically with the available options, and reflects on the choices we made, and the way we handled issues of justice. To put it in another way, consensus has to be created on what is just in a context; it is not pre-given and it cannot be taken for granted. We have also to question the judgments we habitually make, often unreflectively, about what is just and unjust. It is exercises of this kind that are deeply political, that need to be invigorated and brought in centrally into the discussions and thinking about justice.

The Uttarakhand floods saw three different responses, and even more importantly, none of these responses drew upon settled ways of distributing goods within a community. While caste and community organizations may have stepped in, the response of an overwhelming number of people as well as governments at the centre and the states did not determine the fate of the people on the basis of their caste position or community affiliation. All of them alluded to some democratic principles of governance that did not directly rely on notions of caste hierarchy.

The first, most immediate, response that came from the state and society focused on the plight of the pilgrims that were stranded either at the Temple of Kedarnath or on their way to that destination. Since the Temple was located at a greater height and the area around it was affected gravely, there was good reason for fixing attention upon them. But there was perhaps more to it than just this. There were people living in that area who were also affected but the media – 24 X 7 news channels – were concerned about the plight of the pilgrims who were headed towards Kedarnath. The response of the state was, to some extent, understandable: since the Indian state frequently facilitates the organization of religious festivals and tries to ensure that people are able to perform what they regard to be important religious practices, their effort to assist the pilgrims first was only to be expected. The response of the media and the middle class probably stemmed from a different thinking. In a society that is becoming more and more mobile the fate of the people traveling to a region – that is, who happened to be there – connected with the middle classes everywhere (and this included the media, bureaucracy, and the government). The pilgrims may have made a choice to travel to this region, but the flash floods had not been predicted and they certainly did not choose that. The internal logic of a pilgrimage was also ignored by them: the fact that a pilgrimage is meant to be an arduous journey, with apparent risks and dangers that are a reminder of the challenges that we confront in everyday life, was not considered seriously. What seems to have struck a chord is that these people were away from the safety and security of their home, and this is what made them the most vulnerable or the worst-off. Attention could turn to those living in the region in the days that followed, ostensibly on the same ground.

The moral intuition was guided by the belief that home, and to some extent being with one's family, was an important consideration for human life. Although at the most general level their understanding of justice rested on the need principle and expressed the view that all the affected persons had to be (and would be) rescued/assisted, the gaze rested first and foremost on travelers to the region, many of whom were also pilgrims. Liberals often make a distinction between choice and circumstance: the state, they argue, has no obligation to provide for the lifestyle I chose, or the choices

I make – like playing golf or driving a fast car – but it must compensate those who face a disadvantage on account of the circumstances they are placed in or born into. This reasoning which frequently guides distribution of social goods offered little guidance in this situation. Indeed it was difficult to make the distinction between choice and circumstance on this occasion. At one level those traveling to the region had made a choice: they decided to visit this region at that time. Yet no one had made the choice to travel at a time when there was a risk of sudden floods. So even if we accept that they made a choice, it was not a decision based on full information, and hence not a choice that we should hold them to. The predicament of the people living in the region was equally complicated. They happened to be living there; it was not a choice they made. Residents of the region could of course leave and settle elsewhere, so if they continue to stay in Uttarakhand, one might say that they made a choice to live there – that is, live in the region which is ecologically fragile. But did they really have this choice? They were born into families whose life and livelihood were tied to that region, and the opportunities for living elsewhere were extremely limited. In any case the environmental crisis that triggered flash floods was not of their making alone. Others, those living outside the region, had contributed to it. Either way, the hard issue of who should be rescued first could not be settled by drawing upon the distinction between choice and circumstance. At the same time the matter could not also be decided on the basis of either community solidarity or ritual hierarchy. The logic that defines democracy – that is, as citizens all persons should be treated alike – was invoked to underline the obligation that the state has towards all the affected persons. But beyond that, who should be rescued on a priority basis was understood differently.

A different response came from the then Chief Minister of Gujarat. He made special arrangements to rescue and bring back the stranded Gujarati tourists/pilgrims from the region. This response rested on the belief that elected leaders particularly have a responsibility towards their electorate. This is not an uncommon or indefensible assumption in a democracy. In fact the electorate appeals to, and petitions, the elected leader to stand up for them and make an effort to protect their interest. In many situations involving crisis of different kinds, natural or political, citizens appeal to their heads of state for assistance. In the landslide that occurred at Leh, for instance, foreign nationals got assistance from representatives of their government and they were evacuated on a priority basis by the latter. Different governments took care of their citizens. Yet, the decision made by the Chief Minister of Gujarat sent alarm bells ringing.

The response of the Gujarat Chief Minister too was impelled by a consideration that prevails in a democracy. It did not invoke a community's tradition or self-understanding; it focused on the obligation of an elected government towards its people. However, it made a distinction between citizens; in place of using the nation-state as the relevant unit, it focused on the region. Those who did not agree with this decision believed, at least implicitly, that within the nation-state privileging and attending to the needs of one's own electoral constituency was indefensible. Since in crisis of a similar kind (as in the case of Leh) few people objected to countries rescuing their own citizens first, one can assume that most accepted the distinction between citizens and noncitizens/foreign citizens; they were dissatisfied with the internal distinctions made between people belonging to different regions within the country.

Many theorists of distributive justice maintain that redistribution of goods requires the existence of a bounded community; it needs some degree of trust between members, a sense of commonality and a shared identity. In the present world, they feel, that it is the nation-state that can, and does, nurture this form of identity and belonging (Canovan 1996). One might have some sense of obligation towards all of humanity, but it is exceedingly difficult to sustain a deep sense of solidarity that agendas of redistribution require, at that scale. We know just how difficult it is to arrive at a consensus on matters of redistribution even within a nation-state; to do so on the global scale presents an insurmountable challenge. For these reasons they maintain that it is desirable to take the nation-state as the relevant political unit for questions of justice.

In his book *A Theory of Justice*, John Rawls described society as a system of cooperation. He began with the understanding that some degree of interdependence is a condition of our social life; that is, there are many ways in which our lives are intertwined with those living in the same society. It is this understanding of core dependence that compels us to see ourselves as part of a larger whole and acknowledge our obligations towards each other. Rawls spoke of reciprocity as a condition of our life in society and offered this as a reason for privileging the category of citizenship, and it is from this perspective that the act of rescuing one group of people – people from Gujarat, for instance – seemed improper; after all the survival of these members, and their capacity to travel, was dependent upon the help they received from those living in Uttarakhand and from other tourists and travelers. Mutual dependence and reciprocity needed therefore to be the starting point of discussions on justice.

The same criterion could of course be used to question the distinction between citizens and immigrants in the contemporary world. Even though our fates are closely linked to our fellow citizens, in the globalized world, it is exceedingly difficult to ignore the contributions that noncitizens (living on the same territory) make to our prosperity and well-being. In a global economy people are extremely mobile and through their work they contribute, in complex ways, to the host society. Living for a substantial period of time in another country we also build ties with others around us; at times these ties with the new host society are even more intense and multilayered than with citizens of one's own country. In other words, even if we accept that some boundaries are required for assigning responsibility, one has to consider that the state may have obligations to more than just those who are citizens.

The third response, one that was to some extent used here and in other similar situations, relied on the accepted protocol that we have evolved in recent times: namely, to rescue children, women, the sick, and the elderly first. We have come to see these groups as the most vulnerable although in each society marginalization is not only along these lines. In India the government uses the category of caste and tribe to identify marginalized groups for purposes of distribution of important social goods. A different criterion is however used for identifying vulnerable people in extraordinary situations. In the case of the latter it is young children, women with children, and those with medical conditions that receive priority; they are seen as requiring assistance more than the rest. We know that even within this, for example, among the elderly or among women, the capacity to survive may differ enormously, but the individual counts for less when we consider the normative compulsions of defining what is just. This was an altogether different response; although it did not invoke any specific conception of democracy, it relied on consensus that most states have come to accept in recent times.

By considering the case of Uttarakhand flood, the point I wish to emphasize is that in concrete situations many different moral intuitions are at work. Even in a young democracy like India the idea of what is just is not shaped by the understanding that has prevailed in this society over a long period of time; rather democracy creates new and fresh imperatives which no government can entirely ignore. Within this structure of democracy however different notions of justice surface and they compete with each other by invoking different elements of what democracy entails. It is exceedingly difficult to dismiss any of these ideas as they rely on notions of democracy that we accept in other contexts. In dealing with the question of justice this is the dilemma that we habitually face. No one principle is in itself sufficient and often more than one principle is relevant, and cannot be dismissed summarily. It is for this reason that we need an active public sphere so that these alternative visions of what is just can be discussed and debated in an effort to arrive at some minimum agreement on what a just action might entail in a given situation.

Normative political theory has for long sidestepped this need. It has assumed, rather optimistically, that we can arrive at some principle for constructing a just order that rational individuals can all accept. Unfortunately, reason is not sufficient for arriving at that moment of truth. One has to temper one's expectations, at least in a democracy, and recognize that the only real possibility is to discuss the different frameworks with which we approach a given situation and hope to create a repertoire of, what might be seen as, best practices along with an appreciation of the competing principles that we need to accommodate and make room for in our actions.

References

Canovan, Margaret. 1996. *Nationhood and Political Theory*. Cheltenham: Edward Elgar Publishing

Miller, David. 1999. *Principles of Social Justice*. Harvard, MA: Harvard University Press

Rawls, John. 1971. *A Theory of Justice*. Harvard, MA: Harvard University Press

Walzer, Michael. 1983. *Spheres of Justice: A Defense of Pluralism and Equality*. New York: Basic Books

8 An other theory of justice

Sanjeeb Mukherjee

Political philosophy, since the 1970s, has been dominated by discussions on justice, particularly after the publication of *A Theory of Justice* by John Rawls in 1971. The state, its foundation, its legitimacy and its conduct, has had to face the test of justice. Liberal philosophers like Rawls and Robert Nozick have addressed the question of justice from the perspective of the individual and his rights. Their substantive theories of justice, however, are quite distinct, having major differences – especially on questions of state policy on redistribution. For long, Marxism claimed a certain privilege for primarily keeping alive and addressing the question of justice – social justice, to be more precise. The Marxist understanding of social justice is historicist and structural, that is, according to it injustice is caused by structures of class domination involved in systems of production. Resistance and struggles by the oppressed classes inevitably bring about revolutionary change ultimately leading to the establishment of socialism and communism, which would herald the dawn of justice. This is the law of history.

Can these theories of justice address the catastrophic human situation in overwhelming parts of the world today – endemic starvation, disease, hundreds of millions dying in infancy or before their time, violence and wars or the absence of shelter, clothing and access to clean drinking water on an unimaginably gigantic scale? Or the deaths, injuries and diseases caused by industrial and automobile accidents and the degradation of the environment? This is the situation when knowledge, science and technology have made unprecedented advances, but where only a very tiny section of the global population enjoys unbelievable material prosperity both in the west and in the rest of the world. In this chapter, I shall interrogate the limits of the liberal idea of justice – the limits of the liberal idea of liberty and equality and why these ideas have become "provincial" – European, or Western, in the larger sense of the word – and have failed to address the human condition in the rest of the world, where the overwhelming majority of the people live or why these ideas have not been able to address gigantic historical wrongs – colonialism and capitalism – which went into the making of the modern world or the structures and institutions of economic exploitation which exist all over the world.

DOI: 10.4324/9780429355974-8

Marxists have addressed the structural and historical grounds of injustice but have miserably failed to uphold the rights and dignity of the individual. Liberals are philosophically blind to the cries of the millions for food, shelter, medicine and dignity. Thus, we need to transcend the limits of both these perspectives, at the same time drawing on crucial elements of both to develop a new perspective on justice, which is liberal, in the sense that it upholds individual rights as inviolable, and is at the same time radical, involving a critique of capitalism, and truly universal. This is an overtly ambitious project and in the rest of this chapter, I shall first present a sketch of the global human condition and then I shall briefly comment on the limits of some of the major liberal theories of justice, especially, of John Rawls and Amartya Sen. Sen has drawn our attention to the state of the human condition, and his idea of capabilities does address this situation, but I would argue that if his idea of capabilities is translated into the language of rights, it would be more philosophically sound. I would, to some extent, attempt to do that and work out its implications. In the second part I would try to work out a principle of justice, which is centred on the *right to live, the equal right of every individual to actually live a full and free life.* My argument hinges on a crucial distinction between the liberal *right to life*, which is a mere juridical right, and what I wish to call the *right to live*. In fact, both Hobbes and Locke emphasize on the right to "self-preservation" or the right to live. Then, I shall make a few concluding notes on the nature and implications of this perspective. Finally, by way of an excursus, I shall offer a reading of the amended Indian Constitution, which is close to this principle of justice.

1

The global condition

Philosophers, like mathematicians, in their search for truth, have a fancy for abstraction and a thirst for first principles and foundations. Political philosophers too have followed this hallowed tradition. Liberals have sought to build their first principles upon the hypothetical idea of the state of nature. Now it is generally accepted that the state of nature is not exactly the kind of situation one comes across in real history before the birth of the modern liberal state. It is neither entirely fictive. It posits individuals, individuals in the liberal sense – atomic, rational and selfish, and it also posits patterns of behaviour or thinking of such creatures. This description, though fictive and hypothetical, bears a strong resemblance to the lives and hopes of an actually emerging and articulate middle class or bourgeoisie. Secondly the new state and society to be brought forth will have to evolve principles of justice to address creatures of the above sort. Finally, these descriptions are not only assumptions, they are normative at the same time, indicating the kind of society these philosophers desire.

These assumptions and aspirations gave birth to radically different accounts of the state of nature or the original condition. One where reason, natural law and natural rights existed, and outside Europe where unreason, savagery and barbarism reigned. European liberalism, of course, had a saving grace for the non-western world – it became the white man's burden to civilize the coloured people. This made liberalism a universal doctrine.

My strategy to work out a global theory of justice aims to ask what principles a common person, who is reasonable, would accept, given the actually existing global condition of the people. Amartya Sen and Thomas Pogge, among others, have vividly described the global condition – the condition that any theory must address. I shall schematically reproduce some of the startling statistics from their writings, which in turn is based on primary data drawn from sources like the World Bank and United Nations Development Reports.

2800 million or 46% of the world's population, that is almost half of humanity, live below the World Bank's US $ 2 per day poverty line. Not all of them are equally poor, for 1200 million of them live on less than half, that is, below the World Bank's better-known US $ 1 per day poverty line. Every year 18 million of them die prematurely due to conditions caused by acute poverty. This number is one-third of all human deaths – these deaths can be prevented.[1] About 250 million, mostly children, died in the last 14 years (since the end of the Cold War and the birth of the global era) due to starvation and preventable diseases.[2] According to the Human Development Report 2003 "every day 799 million people in developing countries – about 18% of the world's population – go hungry. In South Asia one person in four goes hungry, and in Sub-Saharan Africa the share is as high as one in three."[3] According to the World Bank two out of five children in the developing world are stunted.[4] According to the World Resources Institute, by 2025 at least 3.5 billion people (nearly 50% of the world population) will face water scarcity. The degradation of the world's fresh water systems threatens all forms of life, human, animal and plant. Diarrhoea, which is caused by poor water quality, causes 2.2 million deaths annually, mostly among children under five. Access to safe water can considerably enhance the chances of survival of children all over the world.[5] Amartya Sen has drawn the world's attention to the millions of "missing women" – women who are killed before they are born or suffer preventable deaths. In 2000 their number was more than 100 million; in China alone it would be more than 50 million and in India 37 million.[6] If Sen were to calculate the missing men, the total figure would truly numb us. In other words, their right to life is grossly violated, of course, not by the state or by any identifiable individual but because of the nature of the social order itself. It has been calculated that the number of people who die in road accidents is more than war casualties. The death and disease caused by environmental degradation are so large that reliable estimates are difficult to make. In spite of the denial of so basic a right as the right to live, they cannot go to a court of law to claim the right to live. To the dominant liberal opinion, these deaths are definitely an embarrassment, but they are not as morally outrageous as the denial of individual freedom or genocide conducted by the state.

Global income distribution is not just unequal, but the proportion of inequality is almost infinite. The 2800 million poor have only 1.2% of aggregate global income, while 903 million people of the high-income economies together have 79.7% share.[7] Income trends under globalization are equally disturbing. According to the World Bank 200 of the world's richest people more than doubled their net worth in four years ending in 1998, to more than $ 1 trillion. The assets of the top three billionaires are more than the combined GNP of all least developed countries and their 600 million people. Today the top quintile of all human beings has around 90% of global income and the bottom quintile one-third of 1%.[8]

2

The right to life

The liberal moral imagination is not perturbed by this state of the world. At best, it addresses these problems in terms of government policies to remove poverty or provide for other forms of social welfare. They are not problematized in the language of justice or rights; rather they are the stuff of governmentality. Poverty and the millions of missing people – men, women and children suffering and dying before their time is something the liberal language of rights is wholly oblivious to. A Solzhenitsyn, a Sakharov, a Salman Rushdie or a Tasleema Nasreen weighs heavily on the liberal moral conscience for they are glaring instances of the denial of human freedom, especially the denial of the freedom to express oneself and one's views and opinions. The Holocaust has become the metaphor of gigantic moral outrages because it was the work of the state, but infinitely larger death counts in history are glossed over when the cause is some impersonal force like the local or global economic and social order.

The conceptual language of liberal justice is the vocabulary of rights, particularly the rights to life, liberty, equality and property. Why cannot the millions of avoidable deaths be treated as a violation or denial of the right to life? But that is not the case. Liberalism has emasculated the meaning of life to a merely *negative juridical category*. Thus Article 5 of the US Constitution states "No person shall be deprived of life, liberty or property, without due process of law". Article 21 of the Indian Constitution says, "No person shall be deprived of his life or personal liberty except according to procedure established by law". Michael Walzer rightly argues that sovereignty, which is the conceptual foundation of the modern state, "does not extend to enslavement; state officials cannot seize the persons of their subjects … or kill them – except in accordance with procedure agreed to by the subjects themselves."[9] Or as Amartya Sen points out "even gigantic famines can result without anyone's libertarian rights (including property rights) being violated".[10]

These are negative rights. They restrain the state from depriving people of their life except under due process of law. Liberty and equality and, to a considerable extent, property have attracted the labour of political philosophers, whereas the right to life has been taken for granted. Most debates surrounding the right to life have centred on the right of unborn babies or the right of their mothers to abort them; the right to life of people on life support systems; or whether capital punishment is just.

However, the early liberal idea of the right to life was far more radical and robust as found in Hobbes and Locke. CB Macpherson in an essay on *Natural Rights in Hobbes and Locke* argues that the Right of Nature, according to Hobbes,

> is the liberty each man hath, to use his own power, as he will himself, for the preservation of his own nature; that is to say, of his own life; and, consequently, of doing anything, which in his own judgement and reason, he shall conceive to be the aptest means thereunto ... . And because the [natural] condition of man ... is a condition of war of every one against every one; ... and there is nothing he can make use of, that may not be a help unto him, in preserving his life against his enemies; it followeth, that in such a condition, every man has a right to every thing, even to one another's body.[11]

Hobbes's argument in favour of the right to life or self-preservation is so radical that in the state of nature, in order to preserve his life, man has a right to everything, "even to another's body". In other words, he upholds every individual's life even at the expense of the other's life or body. This may appear to be a contradiction, but it could be explained by Hobbes's assumption about the state of nature, which in turn, leads to the logical step of setting up a state. Hobbes again writes,

> It is ... a right of nature: that every man may preserve his own life and limbs, with all the power he hath. And because where a man hath a right to the end ... it is consequent that it is ... right for a man, to use all means and do whatsoever action is necessary for the preservation of his body.[12]

Hobbes here categorically uses the phrase "preservation of his body" to make sense of the right to life. The necessary condition of the right to life is the satisfaction of the basic needs of the body – needs without which life or survival is impossible. Macpherson again quotes Hobbes to spell out his position further,

> But because, it is in vain for a man to have a right to the end, if the right to the necessary means be denied him; it follows, that since every man

hath a right to preserve himself, he must also be allowed a right to use all the means, and do all the actions, without which he cannot preserve himself.[13]

Clearly, for Hobbes, the right to life is not a mere juridical or formal right; it is a substantial right.

Locke too maintained that God had planted in man the strongest desire of self-preservation and gave nature to him for his food and other necessaries. God's design was that "man should live and abide for some time upon the face of the earth" and gave him the means of his "preservation". Thus he has the right "to make use of those things that were necessary or useful to his being".[14] Locke adds that since we are all children of God we should not "take away or impair the life, or what tends to the preservation of the life, the liberty, health, limb or goods of another".[15] To Locke the chief end of the state is the "preservation of property" and by property he means "life, liberty and estate".[16] He calls it the "fundamental, sacred and unalterable law of self preservation".[17] In the light of my reading of Locke it becomes clear how actually existing liberalism emasculated the right to life or self-preservation into the juridical right of the state to take away the right to life under due process of law. And citizens as long as they uphold the relevant laws could not be denied the right to life. It thus, for the citizen, became a mere negative juridical right. Self-preservation became a private matter of the individual to pursue. It became subsumed under the rights to liberty and equality. It was assumed that if liberty and equality were guaranteed, individuals would be able to fend for themselves and not being able to do so came to be considered as an individual failure.

The limits of Rawls's theory of justice

Contemporary liberal theories of justice have focused on both, rights – particularly liberty and equality – and, on principles of redistribution and social welfare. Here, again, we should make a distinction between the actually existing liberal states and their working principles of justice and the body of liberal political philosophies of justice, most prominently found in Rawls and Nozick. As I had earlier argued there is a distinction between the liberal state and its principles of justice as found in its constitution, and the government of the day which undertakes major policies and pieces of legislation providing for a diverse range of welfare and redistribution of wealth and income. The government of the day is largely guided by utilitarian principles – providing for the greatest good of the largest number. This utilitarianism of the government does not formally violate rights because it initially identifies and defines a target group worthy of receiving welfare and all those falling in that group by a previously declared criterion becomes eligible for welfare. Hence within that target group, nobody's rights are violated. In fact, such declared definitions and criteria can only defend progressive taxation, which within that group is non-discriminatory. Thus the claim of contemporary liberal political theories of justice to sharply distinguish itself from utilitarianism does not exist in real history. Though there is no constitutional right to welfare in actually existing liberal states, once a government policy on any kind of welfare exists, the concerned people can make rights claims, both substantial, that is, the specific welfare as well as procedural and formal to prevent any discrimination.

John Rawls has formulated the most important and powerful liberal principles of justice. They are:

a) Each person has the same indefeasible claim to a fully adequate scheme of equal basic liberties, which scheme is compatible with the same scheme of liberties for all; and
b) Social and economic inequalities are to satisfy two conditions: first, they are to be attached to offices and positions open to all under conditions of fair equality of opportunity; and second, they are to be to the greatest benefit of the least-advantaged members of society (the difference principle).[18]

Rawls further holds that the first principle is prior to the second and in the second principle fair equality of opportunity is prior to the difference principle.[19]

Rawls's principles appear to be universal which any rational individual anywhere in the world could accept. A reading of these principles assumes that people's basic need of survival and physical well-being is either taken care of or such needs do not constitute the subject of justice. Justice is something loftier than bread and milk. Justice seems to only address moral issues like liberty, formal equality or even some redistribution principles. Rawls, however, himself clarifies these problems by spelling out his presuppositions and preconditions for his two principles of justice to operate.

Rawls admits that he is "mainly concerned with ideal theory: the account of the well-ordered society of justice as fairness".[20] Though he claims his theory to ignore "historical facts", I would try to show that his theory presupposes and privileges a particular historical setting – that of the western world. In *Political Liberalism*, Rawls clearly says:

> The last point about the priority of liberty is that this priority is not required under all conditions … . it is required under what I shall call "reasonably favourable conditions," that is, under social circumstances which, provided the political will exists, permit the effective establishment and the full exercise of these liberties. These conditions are determined by a society's culture, its traditions and acquired skills in running institutions, and its level of economic advance (which need not be especially high) and no doubt by other things as well. I assume as sufficiently evident for our purposes, that in *our country today* reasonably

favourable conditions do obtain, so that *for us the priority of the basic liberties is required.*[21]

(Emphasis added)

Rawls quite categorically lays down conditions for his theory of justice which are clearly not universal; rather they are quite firmly located in the west. In fact, his description of "the circumstances of justice" reflects "the historical conditions under which *modern democratic societies* exist. These include .... the objective circumstances of *moderate scarcity* and the necessity of social cooperation for all to have a decent standard of life"[22] (emphasis added). If we recall our description of the global condition in the beginning of this chapter, we would find that these conditions or circumstances are absent in most parts of the world and for most people residing outside the "*modern democratic* societies". Their condition, very succinctly, is a situation of acute scarcity and a striving for the bare minimum in order to survive.

Not that Rawls is oblivious of the basic needs of humankind or what he calls "primary goods", but the status he assigns to these primary goods is problematic, especially if we view them as absolutely necessary not only for the west but for the whole of humankind. The Enlightenment rationality-inspired liberalism's claim to universality soon reaches its limits when the fine print of some of the major arguments is closely examined. The contradictions, the qualifications, the ambiguities, the hesitancy or even the moral embarrassment come out quite sharply in the writings of Rawls. There is a sense of a deep moral discomfort in liberalism, a discomfort that it is unable to address. This makes liberalism parochial. The common reaction in the non-western world is to reject liberalism for its inability to address its own circumstances of justice. After examining Rawls, I would attempt to offer a radical modification in liberal principles of justice to make it universal, to enable it to address the circumstances of justice prevailing in most parts of the world.

Rawls claims his theory to be "ideal" and thus he ignores "historical facts". In fact, his theory does admit the necessity of meeting basic human needs through what he calls "primary goods". He resolves the problem of primary goods in two ways, first, by definition he imagines the initial situation where primary goods are available to everybody and hence is not the issue of justice. Secondly, he also admits to a historical divide between well-ordered and well-endowed modern democratic societies where primary goods are taken care of, and the rest of the world. Justifying primary goods, Rawls says

> that it is rational to want these goods whatever else is wanted, since they are in general necessary for the framing and the execution of a rational plan of life. The persons in the original position are assumed to accept this conception of the good.

It includes "liberty and opportunity, income and wealth, and above all self-respect". He adds that primary goods serve "as part of the description of the initial situation. The reason is, of course, that this list is one of the premises from which the choice of the principles of right is derived".[23]

By including primary goods as part of the initial situation he makes another major explicit departure from his well-known deontological philosophical position which posits the priority of the right over the good. Thus Rawls holds that "The constraints of the principles of justice cannot be used to draw up the list of primary goods" in the "initial situation". He adds,

> At no point can we appeal to the constraints of justice. But once we are satisfied that the list of primary goods can be arrived at in this way, then *in all further applications of the definition of the good the constraints of right may be freely invoked.*[24]
>
> (Emphasis added)

In the face of a lot of criticism, Rawls later revises his position on the status of primary goods in his theory of justice consisting of his famous two principles. He writes in *Political Liberalism*:

> Finally, as one might expect, important aspects of the principles are left out in the brief statement as given. In particular, the first principle covering the equal basic rights and liberties *may easily be preceded* by a lexically prior principle requiring that citizens' basic needs be met, at least insofar as their being met is necessary for citizens to understand and to be able fruitfully to exercise those rights and liberties. Certainly any such principle *must be assumed* in applying the first principle.[25]
>
> (Emphasis added)

Rawls's understanding of primary goods is merely as a means, which is necessary to exercise rights and liberties. Of course, that is what it should normally be, otherwise the moral superiority of human beings over animals becomes suspect. But what about people who are unable to exercise their rights, say being physically or mentally challenged or even children? Will they be provided for the basic needs, which alone will enable them to live? Is life, *per se*, sacred and of such value, that it has to be preserved? Or is life merely a means to exercise liberty and other rights? As Rawls[26] moves from a moral and philosophical theory of liberalism to a *political* conception of liberalism he does not address the moral worth of human life itself. Rawls now claims his principles of justice are even egalitarian and hence are not merely formal. The difference principle, which though, he admits, is not part of the constitutional essentials, takes care of equality.[27] However, when it comes to real historical situations marked by acute scarcity and gross inequalities Rawls takes a position, which, I would argue, is grossly biased against the situation existing in the non-western world. He writes,

> *in the absence of special circumstances*, it seems wrong that some or much of society should be amply provided for, while many, or even a few, suffer hardship, not to mention hunger and treatable illness. ... *unless there is real scarcity*, all should have at least enough to meet their basic needs.[28]
>
> (Emphasis added)

The qualifications Rawls introduces for accepting hunger is "special circumstances" or "real scarcity", both of which are extremely tricky and morally problematic.[29] In fact, when he explicitly discusses the principles of global justice, Rawls maintains that:

> There should be certain provisions for mutual assistance between peoples in times of famine and drought, and were it feasible, as it should be, provisions for ensuring that *in all reasonably developed liberal societies* people's basic needs are met.[30]
>
> (Emphasis added)

When he talks of the global situation, his dictum about meeting people's basic needs in difficult situations is confined to only all "reasonably developed liberal societies". I think the kind of morally problematic stand that Rawls takes in times of famine or acute scarcity – which is often the case in large parts of the world – is due to his privileging of the moral personality or self whose central concern is liberty and other rights. For life to exist the basic needs of the human body have to be addressed, and these needs can only be prioritized if human life itself is given supreme importance and worth. Rawls's concept of the self has generated a major debate and in an earlier chapter I entered that debate to problematize some of its presuppositions. Here, again, I only wish to show that even in the later Rawls's idea of the free and equal person and his or her "two moral powers" he makes a crucial, though implicit, distinction between human life *per se* and "*What is of value in human life* or, alternatively, of what is regarded as a fully worthwhile life"[31] (emphasis added). We had seen earlier that primary goods are necessary to fruitfully exercise rights and liberties especially in "reasonably developed liberal societies".

If Rawls had taken a fundamental moral position in favour of the sacredness and worth of human life as such, he would surely have placed basic human needs as the first principle of universal justice. As a liberal he could have added liberty and equality as intrinsic principles of a just human existence. I would be arguing in favour of the right to live in the latter part of this chapter. In other words, if we redescribe primary goods in the language of rights, especially the right to life, then I think it would make a philosophically and morally more stronger case which then could be universally applicable. And given the global condition or the global circumstances of justice, prioritizing life would make better moral sense.

I now wish to, very briefly, attempt an interpretation of why the shift took place in the first principles of liberal justice from Hobbes and Locke to Rawls and Nozick – a shift from self-preservation or life, liberty and equality to only liberty and equality. The crucial change came about as a result of the Kantian privileging of reason and morality in the definition of the self. Contemporary liberalism bases itself on the Kantian idea of a transcendental self – a rational and moral agency independent of any emotion, desire or bodily needs. Victor Seidler, in an important critique of Kant's social and moral theory, argues that there is a strong Christian influence in considering the body with suspicion,[32] as something which prevents the higher pursuits of our soul. He further argues that in Kant's idea of the self, our dignity lies in our morality whereas our sensible world is a world of determination, governed by the mechanism of equivalence and price. In other words our dignity, our morality and our rationality, all that which defines our essence, are divorced from our body, our emotions and needs.[33] This Kantian notion of the disembodied or unencumbered self[34] explains contemporary liberalism's primary concern with liberty and equality and not with basic human needs or primary goods.

Secondly, liberals do not even address the global situation though their theories claim a universal status because of their strong individualist basis. This again flows from Kant's idea of respect as non-interference or leaving people alone to pursue their own ends and goals.[35] This is premised on the idea of the self as a self-sufficient atom who being rational is responsible for leading a moral life of freedom. Thus comes Kant's maxim, "Each man for himself: God for us all".[36] Seidler therefore argues that in liberalism poverty is seen as a sign of moral inadequacy or as an individual failure.[37] In fact, in actually existing liberal states, liberty and equality are held as trumps over everything else, including the right to live or to survive. Interestingly, though theoretically, most liberals do not hold property to be a right at par with liberty or equality, in actually existing liberal states property is considered to be as invaluable a right as liberty or equality. In fact, liberty is often defined to include property and any violation of the right to property is held to be an infringement on liberty itself. Hence any serious redistribution of property to meet the requirements of basic human needs is ruled out.

Certain important assumptions and certain historical conditions have also changed since the time of Hobbes and Locke. Early liberalism shared the optimistic assumption about nature being bountiful and that there is plenty for all men to acquire and consume and thus survive. Marx too shares this optimism, of course, only after the socialist revolution. In fact, Marxists believe that material abundance under communism would make all liberal rights and justice redundant. Rawls, we had seen, assumes only moderate scarcity and rules out his theory of justice in situations of acute scarcity and want. It is only Gandhi and later on ecologists who have made us aware of the actual global condition of acute scarcity of resources and acute inequality existing simultaneously. And it is this twin condition that any properly universal theory of justice must address.

In spite of a global resource scarcity, western societies, due to the historical conditions created by colonialism and capitalism, have largely solved the problems of acute poverty and human survival. People in large numbers do not die in the west due to starvation or malnutrition or preventable diseases. Capitalism and colonialism enabled the west to forcibly transfer immense human and natural resources from its former colonies. Secondly, the whole population of three continents – the Americas and Australia – was largely decimated and the continents occupied by Europeans. This was human history's most gruesome genocide making America and not Auschwitz the metaphor of genocide. This history must be unveiled and addressed by any theory of justice.[38]

3

Ritwik Ghatak's The Cloud Capped Star *and questions of justice and responsibility*

Bengal in the 1950s and 1960s was in ferment. It saw great works in the world of cinema, music, literature, art and theatre. Satyajit Ray is more internationally known, but his contemporary Ritwik Kumar Ghatak also made some very powerful and disturbing films where he raised crucial questions of justice and responsibility. In this section, I shall discuss one of his films *Meghe Dhaka Tara* or *The Cloud Capped Star* made in 1960. This film, like many of his other works as well, tells the story of a young woman called Nita in the background of larger historical and social forces at work. Nita's family, like millions of others, was turned into refugees after the partition of Bengal in 1947, at the time of Indian independence. In the midst of extreme poverty and deprivation Nita shows exemplary courage and virtue. She gives up her education, her lover and her personal interests to shoulder the responsibility of her old parents and younger siblings. In the face of such trying circumstances her brothers and her sister soon desert their family and familial responsibilities in search of better opportunities. Hard work, personal tragedies and poverty takes a toll on her and she contracts tuberculosis.

Nita's father suffers helplessly, and unable to bear her suffering and exploitation, he wants to intervene. He shouts loudly "I accuse". He obviously wanted to accuse his other children and his wife for exploiting Nita. But he does not complete the sentence, for he not only has to accuse himself but also has to accuse the larger historical forces responsible for the partition of Bengal and their social situation. He stops midway because the juridical category of "I accuse" does not hold for historical and social forces.

Nita showed great courage and virtue in the Levinasian sense of responsibility towards her family. I would argue that Ghatak's film shows the insufficiency of this ethic. This ethic, though necessary, does not work to prevent the tragedy, which befell her. A tragedy which seems inevitable, waiting to unfold itself because of the consequences of larger historical forces at play in the structures and processes of colonialism and capitalism.

Ritwik Ghatak's protagonists like Nita fail not because of a lack of responsibility but because they could not engage with the larger structural forces of world history. Ritwik Ghatak, being a Marxist, shows the importance of both, a sense of responsibility and the necessity to engage with historical forces. This is in sharp contrast with Satyajit Ray's heroes, especially in his famous Apu trilogy where the individual hero through courage, will and optimism triumphs over tragedies which are entirely personal; untouched by history.

Ghatak's film, though it ends in personal tragedy, actually asserts an optimism. Her brother, since having left them, succeeds in life and returns home to find his sister, Nita, in a serious condition. He takes her to a sanatorium in the mountains but is unable to save her. The film ends by Nita's impassioned cries, helplessly declaring to her brother, "*Dada*, I wanted to live!" "*Dada*, I'll live!" and "*Dada*, I loved life very much!".

Nita asserts her indomitable desire and will to live in the midst of the most trying circumstance; in fact, in the face of death itself. Her death only proves how important and fundamental is the right to live. I had earlier introduced the concept of the social existence forms of ideas. In this film, we find the protagonist realizing the supreme value of life in the face of death – an idea she existentially discovers. The audience of the film, too, comes to share this elementary, yet profound discovery. The will, the urge and the desire to live is a profound moral and existential truth, which is exemplified in Nita.

This realization of the sacredness and supreme value of human life is as old as human civilization. The Bible says, "Thou shalt not kill".[39] The Buddhist primer, the Dhammapada, says something having much stronger and wider implications about both our right to live and the responsibility we have towards others. It says, "Do not kill or cause to kill".[40] Gandhi also says:

> Every human being has a right to live and therefore to find the wherewithal to feed himself and where necessary, to clothe and house himself.[41]

This idea is part of the popular consciousness of the poor and thus they often ask, "Don't we have the right to survive?"[42] Unfortunately, an idea, which exists in so many popular forms, is absent in contemporary liberal or even radical theories of justice in any serious sense. In fact, Locke brings an important issue when discussing the right to life and survival by bringing in the question of the responsibility we owe to the rest of mankind.

Amartya Sen's Idea of Justice: *a critique*

Attempts have been made to address some of these difficulties in the global condition where contemporary liberal theories of justice have failed. Amartya Sen, Thomas Pogge and Martha Nussbaum have argued the most influential alternatives. I shall first briefly examine Sen's thesis and then offer my principle of justice. Most of these alternative liberal accounts of justice focus on basic human needs, functionings and capabilities. Many of these have also been accepted by the United Nations since the Second World War, in the form of the Universal Declaration of Human Rights, the International Covenant on Economic, Social and Cultural Rights, the International Covenant on Civil and Political Rights, children's rights, the Right to Development and the Millennium Development Goals. The major thrust of this approach has been to translate human needs in the language of rights – the rights to food, shelter, health, education or work.

Amartya Sen's perspective is the most radical one and I would argue that there is a tension in Sen between the human needs perspective and the perspective of valuing and upholding life itself. I shall argue in favour of prioritizing life itself. My prioritizing of life itself is based on a crucial distinction between the means required and the end – human needs and human life. Sen starts by making a critique of the "priority of liberty" perspective in contemporary liberal theories of justice. He asks, "Why should the status of intense economic needs, which can be matters of life and death, be lower than that of personal liberties?"[43] In this context he gives the example of famine, when "even gigantic famines can result without anyone's libertarian rights (including property rights) being violated … . Similarly, deprivation of other types … can coexist with all libertarian rights … being fully satisfied."[44] It should, however, not be assumed that Sen therefore upholds the priority of basic human needs over liberties much like the standard way the liberal-Marxist divide is made out to be – bread vs. freedom.

Sen makes an important move by redescribing his perspective as the "radical nature of the idea of development as freedom".[45] Sen defines development as the "removal of major sources of unfreedom: poverty as well as tyranny, poor economic opportunities as well as systematic social deprivation, neglect of public facilities as well as intolerance or overactivity of repressive states."[46] To him development is expansion of "substantive freedoms". He further enumerates five types of freedom, which he investigates in his book. They are "(1) political freedoms, (2) economic facilities, (3) social opportunities, (4) transparency guarantees and (5) protective security".[47]

I would argue that Sen redefines freedom into an all-inclusive category ranging from liberal liberties to basic economic needs. He questions the binary freedom vs. bread by including bread as constitutive of freedom. It, of course, has extremely important implications for real life and social policies; but both for analytical as well as moral reasons, I would prefer to look beyond the binary of freedom vs. bread and introduce a third term, that is, human life itself. Of course, bread and freedom are the crucial means and modalities of life; but sometimes there is something more, which I shall soon discuss. Sen's concept of justice is based on the idea of the "expansion of the 'capabilities' of persons to lead the kind of lives they value – and have reason to value".[48] Later, he defines "substantive freedoms" as the capability to "choose a life one has reason to value".[49]

In *The Idea of Justice* Sen admits the importance of the "the centrality of human lives" and the freedom to "live reasonably long lives" or the "freedom to choose different kinds of lives" (Sen 2009, p 225ff). He of course recognizes the importance of rights as an "ethical assertion" (p 359) or a moral claim. For analytical and moral purposes I would distinguish between the intrinsic value of human life, and what Sen calls the "capabilities" of persons "to lead the kind of lives they value – and have reason to value". The importance of this distinction becomes evident when we see the large-scale destruction of human lives – lives of children or the unborn girl child or the physically or mentally challenged or the old, infirm or sick – who often are unable to express or even form the capabilities to lead the kind of life they value, let alone have any reason or are able to offer any reason for the life they would value. Are their lives important and valuable? Do they have the right to actually live? Or do they just enjoy the liberal juridical right to life which means that the state cannot take away their lives, without the due process of law? Does human life have an intrinsic moral worth and hence is entitled to certain rights whether the person concerned is either capable of valuing it or offering reasons for it?

The intrinsic moral worth of human life has been upheld by civilizations and religions. Thus it is not merely a question of choosing a "life one has reason to value". My contention is that it is important to assert the intrinsic moral worth of human life for which no reasons need to be offered. It is a fundamental moral axiom and is neither a matter of choice or of reason. And that is how it exists in most moral thought and in most religions. If the magnitude of human suffering and death in the world, caused by both poverty and wars and violence, has to be addressed, then the priority of the right to live has to be asserted in the first place. In fact, when Sen says that famines or other deprivations can coexist with all libertarian rights being fully satisfied he obviously does not hold the right to live to be a fundamental liberal right which is violated. Therein lies the significance of the right to live.

Sen's concept of capabilities focuses on "the person's ability to promote her ends".[50] My argument makes a distinction between the person and her ends – the person first has to be alive, and as I pointed out earlier there are many cases where she is unable to choose or even define her ends. The ends and the choices and reasons are, of course, crucial; but prioritizing the end over the person is morally unsustainable. I had earlier mentioned a tension in Sen between his privileging of human capabilities and upholding life itself. For example, he does write about "a very elementary freedom: the ability to survive rather than succumb to premature mortality". He adds, "This is, obviously, a significant freedom, but there are many others that are also important".[51] He thereby undermines the priority of life itself.

4

The right to live

Thus, I wish to argue for the *right to live* as the foundation of justice. But not only that, for what kind of life is one without freedom or equality. Political philosophers have proposed different hierarchies of values, some privileging freedom, others equality or even community. Likewise it could be asked what the value of liberty or equality is when you are unable to actually survive or live. I would thus propose the following principle of justice, which, I claim, is universal:

The equal right of every person to actually live a full and free life

This principle incorporates three fundamental liberal rights of every individual – the right to liberty, the right to equality and the right to live. As I pointed out earlier, actually existing liberalism has upheld life, liberty, equality and property. The right to life meant only a juridical right, which prevented the state from denying the right to life without due process of law. Whereas the *right to live* is a positive statement – the right to actually live, live a free, full and equal life. This principle imposes an obligation on the state to provide whatever is necessary for every individual to live a full, free and equal life. Amartya Sen raises a vital question about equality. He argues that every ethical doctrine asks "why equality?"; the important point is to enquire into the key question about "equality in some space, requiring equal treatment of individuals in some significant respect" – it could be liberties or income or utilities. In other words, according to Sen, the crucial issue becomes "equality of what?"[52] My answer to the question "equality of what?" would be: *The equal right of every person to actually live a full and free life*. Put simply, we have an equal right to live. I however wish to privilege the right to live only in the last resort, for example, during grave emergencies liberty could be temporarily curtailed, but never the right to live. In other words, the right to live should be treated as a "political trump" in Ronald Dworkin's sense of the term, that is, "Individuals have rights when, for some reason, a collective goal is not a sufficient justification for denying them what they wish, as individuals, to have or to do, or not a sufficient justification for imposing some loss or injury upon them."[53]

I would add that when a person is *unable* to prioritize any right her right to live is unconditional and absolute overriding all other considerations – both collective goals and other individual rights. Thus, if an individual wishes to exercise her libertarian rights in such a way that jeopardizes her life itself, she is fully free to do so. In other words, the state is not morally entitled to curb her liberties to protect her rights in such instances. This makes the right to live an independent and antecedent principle of justice.

Kant argues that man is an end in himself because he is capable of morality. The sensible world is a world of determination where everything has an equivalence and a price. On the other hand, human morality based on reason admits of no equivalence. Thus it has a dignity and not a price. This makes all men equally worthy of respect. Thus Victor Seidler[54] argues that this identification of the moral with the rational and the universal makes for a fragmented concept of the self – a noumenal and transcendental disembodied self divorced from our bodily needs, emotions and social relationships. Seidler offers a moral theory of human needs.[55] As I argued earlier, I would make a distinction between human life and its needs; not because life can exist without its means or wherewithal, but because due to moral and analytical reasons human life *per se* has to be given a supreme or absolute priority. It is a *moral* axiom not dependent on reason. Of course, reasons can be offered, but they are neither necessary nor sufficient. In fact, if human life is taken to be an end in my sense then it could be a foil to any argument which might try to justify, in very special circumstances, the denial of the right to live, for example, even during wars civilian lives can, in no circumstances, be violated.

Liberal theories of justice presuppose a reasonable individual in the hypothetical state of nature who would rationally arrive at some basic principles of justice and these invariably have been liberty and formal equality, including some schemes of distributive justice to benefit the least advantaged as found in Rawls (1971). This construct of the reasonable individual is no simple thought experiment oblivious of history and the real conditions of existence. When almost half of the global population live below the poverty line and a large proportion of them live in conditions of acute poverty, malnutrition, disease and premature death; what principles would they choose? Liberty, formal equality, property or life itself, a right to equally live a free and full life, that is, not die prematurely or not be able to ensure the survival of their children. Such people would also ask why their condition is so abysmal in spite of the miraculous developments and achievements of science, technology and medicine. Or why do people in the west have such disproportionate amounts of wealth and power, and control most of the land and resources of the globe? This inquiry would take them to what happened in history, especially recent history – the history of colonialism, imperialism and neocolonialism, which is responsible for the current situation. Such people would proceed from knowledge of history and not wear a veil of ignorance. Thus the assumptions and thought experiments of the standard liberal theories of justice are not as hypothetical and innocent as they claim. Their assumption of the reasonable individual is far from universal; they are steeped in Europe's history, power and interests including their permanent settlements outside Europe.

It is not that the west denies its citizens the right to live, rather their survival and general well-being, especially of the whites, are guaranteed by their economic order and some appropriate state policies. Since their lives are not threatened, it is not incorporated as a fundamental right or principle of justice.

In fact, if there is one right, which is truly universal it is the right to life or to be more precise, the right to live. Every culture, community and religion has expressed a fundamental faith in the sanctity or sacredness of human life. Of course, not everybody would respect the life of people outside their community or religion. But today, in the time of globalization, would anybody deny the universal status of the right to live? It does not have to be ontologically or epistemologically grounded; it is part of our instinctive moral sense. It is morally self-evident. And human beings are moral, they have a moral sense.

The right to live may not be always explicitly acknowledged but an implicit agreement can be discerned. In fact, a common refrain, expressed by the poor and the victims of suffering, is "Don't we have a right to live?" In fact, the right to live is violated on such a gigantic scale all over the globe that a universal convention on the right to live needs to be held and any violation should be treated as a crime against humanity. A global commission and a global court should be set up to make this right justiciable and enforceable and its violation severely punishable. More people have died of want, hunger and disease in human history. These deaths, at least today, can be prevented.

For the right to live to be actually realized, one needs many other entitlements – especially to lead a free and full life of dignity and respect. Among others, it entails livelihood, family, culture and community. If the basic institutions of society like the market and modes of production, the means of communication, states and nations are judged on the criteria of our principle of justice, namely, the equal right of all persons to live a free and full life, then the whole of the global order can be questioned and reformed accordingly, particularly, forces and institutions like capitalism, nationalism or state sovereignty and private or state ownership of natural resources including land.

If my principle of justice is accepted, then all cases of criminal neglect including accidents leading to permanent injury or death could be rectified or held accountable. In the west this is largely the case, but in large parts of the non-western world, even in liberal democratic polities like India, millions of people die preventable deaths, and deaths for which no one is legally accountable because of the absence of the right to live in the positive sense of the term. Such criminal neglect leading to death is accepted almost like fate or destiny. It has been seen that when cultures and communities are undermined and livelihoods destroyed people are marginalized and made into destitutes. Under such conditions of poverty and disempowerment people even lose their ability to resist and fall prey to disease and wretchedness and are actually unable to live their lives fully or freely. Here I wish to make a distinction between employment and livelihood. Amartya Sen rightly points out the far-reaching impact of unemployment on psychological well-being, motivation, self-confidence, family and social life, etc. All of this can largely or entirely be mitigated by alternative sources of employment. But by livelihood I mean occupations, which are not merely sources of income but ways of life including culture and community. Thus when people lose their livelihood and are often simultaneously displaced, they suffer a far greater, often an irreparable social, cultural, economic and psychological loss. Large dams, like the one in Narmada in India, have been the focal point of a major movement, which has brought these issues to the forefront.

Besides poverty, ecological disasters and loss of culture and community, which destroys lives and livelihoods, war is another immediate and direct cause of the denial of the right to life itself. If the right to live is upheld as a "political trump", then no government can get away with war, which causes anybody's death, especially the death of civilians and the destruction of their property, which today is passed off as merely collateral damage. Today the global order is sufficiently efficient and viable in protecting property including intellectual property but has no concern when lives are lost. In the liberal moral imagination private property has occupied centre stage whereas peoples' lives, especially in the non-western world, has no value. Thus it is crucially important to uphold the right to live as the key principle of justice under conditions of increasing globalization. States and companies have to be held responsible for any violation of this key tenet of justice.

The right to live is a sufficiently inclusive category, which has far greater moral and philosophical strength than other ways of addressing human suffering on a global scale. In fact the right to live provides the first principle and moral foundation to the existing attempts to address this question.

Conclusion

Making the impossible possible: here and now

Ideas exist in many different social forms – in popular sayings or in people's consciousness or as part of their common sense and embedded in everyday practices. However, we generally believe that only philosophers and thinkers can produce and properly handle ideas. We had seen that the popular idea and deep moral belief that human life is precious or sacred and that everybody is simply entitled to live is an idea almost as old as civilization itself. But then why do we need to reiterate the same as the first principle of justice? Or, if we need to uphold it, how exactly do we do it? India's leading philosopher Krishna Chandra Bhattacharyya[56] recognized the importance of ideas pulsating in the minds and lives of the common people. He advised India's English-educated intellectuals to not only lead and teach the masses but to learn from them as well. Political philosophy, if it has to centrally address human suffering, has to devise acceptable principles of justice. These principles, of course, do not offer a simple formula; as Amartya Sen puts it, "The greatest relevance of ideas of justice lies in the identification of patent injustice, on which reasoned agreement is possible, rather than in the derivation of some extant formula for how the world should be precisely run."[57]

Though man is mortal (or precisely because of it) preventable human suffering and death is the central issue justice must address. Thus it must uphold and celebrate life, actual living – the equal right of every person to actually live a full and free life. And there is no formula to life. Life is inexhaustible, indescribable and undefinable: making it invaluable. Life is impossible.

If life is impossible, so is justice and that's what makes justice utopian. If justice is impossible and utopian, is there any hope? The impossible can only be aspired and aimed at if the limits of the possible are challenged and transgressed. Human history bears vivid evidence of striving for the impossible and breaking the bounds of the possible. Slavery, colonialism or women's subjugation was in earlier times thought to be natural and hence unalterable. Jacques Derrida's philosophy looks for limits and aporias not in order to become immobile and passive but he deconstructs these limits in order to desire unimagined possibilities. John Caputo calls it "a passion for the impossible"[58] Drucilla Cornell argues that "deconstruction, understood as the philosophy of the limit, gives us the politics of utopian possibility".[59] In fact, she says:

> Throughout this book, I will suggest that the central difference between liberal analytic jurisprudence and deconstruction lies in their divergent opinions on the desirability and possibility of thorough going social and legal transformation. This difference turns on what I will describe as the unreasonable moment of utopianism which is inherent in "deconstruction" and in the writing of Emmanuel Levinas on the ethical relation. The liberals such as Rawls and Nagel are undoubtedly more suspicious of utopianism.[60]
>
> The liberal idea of rights contains inexhaustible possibilities, including utopias. Even a sober liberal like Rawls says
>
> We view political philosophy as realistically utopian: that is, as probing the limits of practicable political possibility.[61]

He adds:

> the problem here is that the limits of the possible are not given by the actual, for we can to a greater or lesser extent change political and social institutions, and much else.[62]

Robert Nozick, considered by critics to be a conservative libertarian, has, in fact, philosophically defended all imagined utopias, of course, subject to certain basic principles of right. Let me quote Nozick on his vision of "a framework for utopia":

> there will not be *one* kind of community existing and one kind of life led in utopia. Utopia will consist of utopias ... Utopia is a framework for utopias, a place where people are at liberty to join together voluntarily to pursue and attempt to realize their own vision of the good life in the ideal community but where no one can *impose* his own utopian vision upon others. The utopian society is the society of utopianism.[63]

Hence liberalism like postmodernism has the potential of dreaming for the impossible and translating it into principles of justice.

The poverty, want, degradation and oppression in most parts of the globe often seem to be unchangeable – there is nothing that can be done except hoping for a Malthussian cure or at best sending some food aid in grave situations like famines or civil wars. It has been calculated that a small shift in global incomes and profits can remove acute poverty from the face of the earth. Thomas Pogge argues that shifting only 1% of aggregate global income to people below the poverty line would eradicate severe poverty worldwide.[64] According to the United Nations World Development Report 1999[65] for $40 billion, basic health and nutrition, basic education, water, sanitation, reproductive health and family planning could be extended to the entire world's population. It says that a yearly contribution of 1% of the wealth of the two hundred richest people (about $7 billion) could provide universal access to primary education. Five per cent would pay for all the basic social services. According to William Tabb[66] a Tobin Tax on all international financial transactions would raise $45 billion a month. Thus money is not the problem. Similarly the Millennium Development Goals aim to address major forms of deprivation in a time-bound frame. This makes the impossible not only possible but practicable.

However, the problem with all these prescriptions and initiatives is that they are advocated as matters of state policy. My elementary principle of justice seeks to translate policies as well as human needs in the language of justice – as an inviolable and fundamental right to live. The European Enlightenment in its attempt to ground every belief in reason, secularism and individual self-interest could not privilege human life for its own sake nor could it demand everybody's responsibility towards everybody else. Liberalism privileges the individual as an independent atom whose responsibility is limited to non-interference in other people's affairs, especially their rights. Everybody is responsible for himself or herself and not for anybody else. Thus liberal ideas of justice can remain unperturbed about human suffering and death on such a gigantic global scale. Thus my elementary principle of justice has to be complimented by the ethical imperative of responsibility towards the other as propounded by Emmanuel Levinas. He says:

it is impossible to free myself by saying "It's not my concern". There is no choice, for it is always and inescapably, my concern. This is a unique "no choice", one that is not slavery.[67]

He perhaps adds this to calm facile liberals. Elsewhere he talks about:

everyman's responsibility toward all others, a responsibility which has nothing to do with any acts one may really have committed. Prior to any act, I am concerned with the other, and I can never be absolved from this responsibility.[68]

This ethic, I hope, would realize my elementary principle of justice, which is liberal, yet radical.

Postscript

There is more than an adequate theory of justice right under our noses, but unfortunately, we have not taken notice of it. I would read the much-amended Indian Constitution, both in letter and spirit, as incorporating the principle of justice I had described earlier. However, I did not arrive at this principle by reading the Constitution, but by journeying through the writings of Rawls, Nozick, Sandel, Sen, etc. Political philosophers or even students of Constitutional law have not given the attention, which it deserves. We have not treated the Constitution with the seriousness it deserves and it is not only the Government of India, which mistakenly advertises the old pre-amended Preamble. Though the Constitution was fundamentally designed as a liberal document, it had major differences with western liberal constitutions. It starts right with the Preamble, which can be eminently compared with the American and French Declarations. The much-studied Declarations, even Derrida offers a reading, are primarily liberal and republican documents. The Indian Preamble borrows some of their major ideas, but it makes a crucial addition, which is absent in these Declarations. It proclaims the centrality of justice; social, economic and political justice, and it precedes liberty, equality and fraternity in the text.

Secondly, the Constitution has an entire chapter on The Directive Principles of State Policy, which enunciated a series of rights, which would have made the right to live real in a substantial sense. However, it remained unsung, as it was not a justiciable section of the Constitution. It was merely a solemn promise and even Jawaharlal Nehru forgot to redeem the single time-bound commitment to ensure free and compulsory primary education by the year 1960.

The Constitution has been amended more than a hundred times making it appear to be somewhat trivial. Yet, some of these crucial amendments were made to ensure justice. One of the most important amendments was to remove the right to property from the chapter on Fundamental Rights. The second major move was to make the Directive Principles at par with the Fundamental Rights (42nd Amendment) to ensure that legislation making for justice would not be quashed on the ground that it clashes with formal liberty or equality. This, of course, does not mean that these liberal rights have been trampled upon, rather, the right to live has been granted a position as exalted as liberty or equality. This has radical consequences for inaugurating justice in India. Thus we can no longer blame the Constitution for failing to bring about justice; it is we who have failed the Constitution.

Finally, the Supreme Court has often been accused of transgressing its limits and encroaching on other arms of the government. Actually, many of its radical judgements have taken into account the philosophy of the Constitution as inscribed in the Directive Principles and the Preamble making the way for the rights to food, work and education. In other words, the Supreme Court has worked on an understanding of the right to life, which is positive and substantial.

Notes

1 Thomas Pogge, *World Poverty and Human Rights*, Cambridge: Polity Press 2002, p 2.
2 Ibid., p 98.
3 Human Development Report 2003, UNDP, pp 87–88, quoted in PB Nayak, 'Development and Human Rights', *Economic and Political Weekly*, Sep 13, 2003, p 3894.
4 Pogge, *World Poverty* (2002), p 97.
5 M. Pandey, 'Thirsty World', *The Statesman*, April 10, 2001.
6 Amartya Sen, *Development as Freedom*, Delhi: Oxford University Press, 2000, p 104.
7 Pogge, *World Poverty* (2002), p 2.
8 Ibid., p 99.
9 Michael Walzer, *Spheres of Justice: A Defence of Pluralism and Equality*, Oxford: Martin Robertson 1983, p 283f.
10 Sen, *Development* (2000), p 66.
11 C.B. Macpherson, *Democratic Theory: Essays in Retrieval*, Oxford: Clarendon Press, 1973, p 225f, from Hobbes, *Leviathan* (Macpherson edition 1968), Chap 14, pp 189f.
12 Ibid., p 226 quoted from Hobbes, *Elements of Law Natural and Political* (Tonnies edition 1889), I Chap 14, Sects, 6–7.
13 Ibid., p 226 quoted from Hobbes, *Philosophical Rudiments concerning Government and Society* (Lamprecht edition), 1949, Chap 1, Sec. 8.
14 John Locke, *Two Treatises of Government*, edited by Peter Laslett, Cambridge: Cambridge University Press, 1967, Book I, Sec. 86.
15 Ibid., Book II, Sec 6.
16 Ibid., Book II, Sec. 6.
17 Ibid., Book II, Sec. 123.
18 Ibid., Book II, Sec. 149.
19 John Rawls, *Justice as Fairness: A Restatement*, edited by E. Kelly, Cambridge, MA: Belknap Press of Harvard University Press, 2001, p 42f. For an earlier version see Rawls, *A Theory of Justice*, Oxford: Clarendon Press, 1972, pp 60f.

116 *Sanjeeb Mukherjee*

20 Ibid., p 43.
21 Ibid., pp 65 & 64.
22 John Rawls, *Political Liberalism*, New York: Columbia University Press, 1993, p 297.
23 Rawls, *A Restatement* (2001), p 84.
24 Rawls, *Theory* (1972), p 433 f.
25 Ibid., p 433f.
26 Rawls, *Liberalism* (1993), p 7; Rawls, *A Restatement* (2001), p 44 fn.
27 Rawls, *Liberalism* (1993), p XVIf.
28 Rawls, *Liberalism* (1993) p 6; Rawls, *Restatement* (2001), p 48.
29 Ibid., p 130.
30 Thomas Pogge and William Tabb show how even a small redistribution of wealth can prevent hunger and want worldwide. See my last section.
31 John Rawls, 'The Law of People', in *Collected Papers*, edited by S. Freeman, Cambridge, MA: Harvard University Press, 1999, p 541.
32 Rawls, *Restatement* (2001), p 18f.
33 Victor J. Seidler, *Kant, Respect and Injustice: The Limits of Liberal Moral Theory*, London: Routledge & Kegan Paul, 1986, p 20.
34 Ibid., p 25.
35 See Chapter 3.
36 Seidler, Kant (1986), pp 56–75.
37 Quoted in Seidler, Kant (1986), p 75.
38 Seidler, Kant (1986), p 78.
39 Robert Nozick, *Anarchy, State and Utopia*, Oxford: Basil Blackwell, 1974. He only mentions what he calls 'the rectification of injustice in holdings' but admits that "I do not know of a thorough or theoretically sophisticated treatment of such issues" (p 152).
40 Sen, *Development* (2000), p 64.
41 Ibid., p 66.
42 Ibid., p 5.
43 Ibid., p 3.
44 Ibid., p 10.
45 Ibid., p 18.
46 Ibid., p 74.
47 Ibid., p 74.
48 Ibid., p 24.
49 Amartya Sen, *Inequality Reexamined*, Oxford: Clarendon Press 1992, p 130.
50 Ronald Dworkin, *Taking Rights Seriously*, London: Duckworth 1977, p xi.
51 Seidler, *Kant* (1986) Chap. III.
52 Ibid., pp 120–123 & Chap. VIII.
53 Sen, *Development* (2000), p 94.
54 Ref. to Narmada.
55 See Krishnachandra Bhattacharyya, '*Swaraj* in Ideas', in *Four Indian Critical Essays*, edited by SK Ghose, Calcutta: Jijnasa, 1977.
56 Sen, *Development* (2000), p 287.
57 John D. Caputo, *The Prayers and Tears of Jacques Derrida: Religion without Religion*, Bloomington: Indiana University Press, 1977. See Introduction.
58 Drucilla Cornell, *The Philosophy of the Limit*, New York: Routledge 1992, p 156.
59 Ibid., p 8.
60 Rawls, *Restatement* (2001) p 4.
61 Ibid., p 5.
62 Nozick, *Anarchy* (1974) p 311f.

63 Ref. to Malthussian theory.
64 Pogge, *World Poverty* (2002), p 2.
65 Quoted in William K. Tabb, *The Amoral Elephant: Globalization and the Struggle for Social Justice in the Twenty-First Century*, Kharagpur: Cornerstone Publications, 2002, p 206.
66 Ibid., p 207.
67 Emmanuel Levinas, 'Ideology and Idealism', in *The Levinas Reader*, edited by S. Hand, Oxford: Basil Blackwell, 1989, p 247.
68 Interview on *Radio Communaute*, 28 Sep. 1982; ibid., p 290.

9 'Oustees' of the contemporary system

Understanding displacement and the idea of justice

R. Umamaheshwari

Even as we deliberate (in a seminar[1]) on whether or not there is any adequate *theory* of justice, *in practice*, each day, the state unfolds a new (market) idea. The latest: *Kayakalp* (*literally* turning around) of the Indian Railways. Ratan Tata will be chairing this reform programme.[2] With land, airways, river and ocean, there is not much left to privatise and occupy, to the detriment of millions; displacement and compensation for it – whether or not just (which will be an afterthought once the 'justice' is meted out) promises to remain the constant refrain. What I wish to do in this chapter is to move away, in fact, from theory into a real world that I have tried to understand in my very limited way: of increasing urban spaces within which also happen to be our universities, government institutions, etc. Perhaps there is need to de-theorise the *form* of what is called justice for the displaced (for whom present systems of justice have just not worked, post-independence, till date); it is important to let their hard, bare truths speak for them, of their oppressions and to build, if possible, not an academic theory, but an alternate thinking paradigm, a discourse, or even a non-theory which has a horizontal, vast and spatially (historically, culturally, politically) expansive inclusive idea of multiple belongingness,[3] multiple identities and multiple political expressions of aspirations which need not necessarily fall into the current R&R (Resettlement and Rehabilitation) jargon, where monetary compensation for removing people from their histories and memories seems to be the inevitable outcome of 'development'. The Xaxa Committee Report (2014) points out that

> Under policy of liberalisation, the effort is to create a climate favourable to investment and this will increase demand for more land than in the past. However, this policy lacks a social thrust. Projects that displace tribal communities by transferring their resources for the development of dominant sections of society can never be development in the true sense. Disproportionately large tracts of land in excess of actual needs have been acquired and CPR diverted for infrastructure projects, mines, dams, and industries, mainly in tribal regions. *This is done for a pittance, without much thought to sharing the fruits of development with*

DOI: 10.4324/9780429355974-9

*weaker sections, particularly tribal DPs/PAPs[4] and the tribal commu-
nity at large ... The State needs to send out a strong message to all its
instrumentalities as well as the corporate sector that there shall be no
forcible and extortionist land acquisition in tribal areas, and that wherever tribal land has to be acquired of necessity, it must be preceded by
comprehensive R&R within a framework of full and free consultation
and tribal participation in development and its benefits in the area of
displacement.*

(Xaxa Committee Report, 2014: 298. Emphasis
mine)

The language of compensation has taken deep roots. And displacement is
necessarily of people in the rural areas, mostly farmers and peasants, craftspeople, artisans and other workers. As David Harvey says – 'Money is
always a form of social power and an instrument of discipline in social
relations rather than a neutral universal equivalent with which to calculate
"welfare-enhancing benefits"' (Harvey, 1999:177).

Three narratives

I share three narratives/discourses from spaces deemed 'marginal'; their concerns, though, are actually central to contemporary political and economic
language of what has turned out to be the 'mainstream'. One of these narratives concerns an idea of justice in another continent and cultural context,
but its background story is similar to the one that 'developing' countries,
such as ours, are grappling with.

  (i.) In the documentary film, titled *In the Light of Reverence*,[5] we find an
interesting example of meanings attached to landscapes and the inherent
language of politics that has dominated America since its formation. The
film presents three contemporary issues of the indigenous/native American
communities – Lakota Sioux, Hopi and Winnemem Wintu – each fighting to protect their sacred mountains and religion against mining/mineral
extraction, recreation/adventure sports against the 'Right' to recreation in
the 'pursuit of happiness', the 'Right' to mine (in pursuit of an occupation) and competing religions. The landscapes of contestation are Devil's
Tower, Hopitutskwa and Mt. Shasta, in each of these cases. One of the
native/indigenous Americans points out (in the film) – 'Native Americans
who have lived on this land for aeons of time are being deprived of the central principle of America, that of religious freedom.' An elderly person from
the Wintu community speaks more forcefully about her right to practise
her religion thus – 'This is my church; I would not go down to your White
people's church and raise hell.' The Lakota author Vine Deloria Jr has this
to say – 'The irony of the situation is that you can go to public land and
ski, you can go on public land, strip a mountain and leave a cyanide *poo*,
but you cannot go on the public land and pray for the earth for continued

fertility!' On the other hand, one of the private miners says – 'They have a right to do anything on public land, so do we have a right to mine.' The native Americans fighting an adventure sports company against climbing their sacred mountain point out that while their sacred places have been defiled time and again, it is still a 'federal crime' to climb the Mt. Rushmore (which symbolises the American colonising history and nationhood), any time of the year.

There are other sites of contestation for the Native Americans. There is a long history of struggle of the Hopi and Navajo people against the U.S. government over the Big Mountain reservation land – since 1882. The Black Mesa in Arizona was where the government allowed mining companies to extract sulphur coal deposits. Over the years, mining activities by private players increased. In the year 1974 the Congress signed a Relocation Act permitting the private company, Peabody Coal and others to use reservation lands of Black Mesa for strip mining. And from then on, the Navajo and Hopi people have been asked to relocate through either pressure or soft trade-offs (money to relocate, etc.). By the 1990s, around 300 families of Navajo and Hopi continued to fight relocation and stood their ground, while filing suits and petitions. On 11 March 1996, a federal judge ruled that Peabody had infringed on human and environmental rights of local people. And that the company's pipeline violated the National Environmental Policy Act and the Surface Mining Control Act and revoked Peabody's mining permit. However, in September the same year, the U.S. Congress passed the Navajo-Hopi Settlement Act, asking the Navajo to relocate by year 2000. In December 2008, the Department of Interior Office of Surface Mining (IOSM) granted a permit to Peabody Coal to continue mining in Black Mesa. The Hopi and Navajo people appealed against the order. A re-evaluation was carried out and the IOSM withdrew the mining permit in the year 2010.[6] The story didn't end there. In the year 2009 the former Chairman of Hopi Nation alleged that the Hopi Tribal Council was co-opted by Peabody Coal. 'Forty individual Hopis have filed a challenge to the U.S. Office of Surface Mining's decision to issue a Life-of-Mine permit to Peabody. The permit would allow Peabody to continue the destructive surface mining for an additional 15 years after 2011.' Economic interests had managed to induce a schism of sorts, leading the Hopi Tribal Council to 'ban' what they called 'environmentalists' for defending their land against mining.

Vernon Masayesva, executive director of Black Mesa Trust and former Hopi Chairman, (said) – 'Of special concern to the Hopi is the continuing drawdown of N-aquifer groundwater and the accidental and deliberate destruction of archaeological sites, burial sites, petroglyphs and other cultural resources'. Klee Benally, Navajo, said – 'My grandmother Roberta Blackgoat once said, "I know each tree, each plant that grows right there. And they know me. The children, grandchildren, great grandchildren need to be right there. We need them to get back to the land and live on our ancestors' land." Until her passing she resisted relocation, still abandoned by the Navajo Nation government, 'unwelcome' by the Hopi Tribal government, and as a testimony to the injustices of US law. As long as I live, I'm not going to sign. [She] continued to demand [Peabody] to stop "destroying the Mother Earth's liver and blood; the coal and the water".[7] (Norrell, 2009)

(ii.) Move over to Odisha. The film, *Mine – Story of a Sacred Mountain*[8] documents the historic battle of the Dongria Konds (a Particularly Vulnerable Tribal Group) with the powerful Vedanta Resources Private Limited Company against bauxite mining on their mountain. The by-now-famous leader of the struggle, Lodu Sikaka looks into the camera and says, 'Niyam Raja is our God, we worship him; we worship the rocks, the hills, our houses and our villages; the mountain is our temple and our god; they want to take the rocks from these mountains; but if they take these rocks away, how will we survive? Because of these mountains, our children live, the rains come, the winter comes, the wind blows, the mountains bring water. If they take away these rocks, we will die; we will lose our soul; *eta Niyamgiri to amar atma* (this Niyamgiri is our soul)!' At the other end, a camera-shy woman, in the midst of her work, points to the other, everyday aspect of the place – 'we grow millets, peas, beans; we grow everything ... we get leaves, *peeri* fruit ... bamboo, roots ...'

Though the Supreme Court upheld the rights of the Dongria Konds and stalled mining on Niyamgiri by an order, over the years, the Dongria Konds are not fully through with the challenges of the system, either. Ashish Kothari writes,

> Niyamgiri, both as a place and as a narrative, needs to be revisited. Enabling the Dongria Kond to decide their own future, based on their understanding of their past and present, requires deep empathy and understanding from anyone outside of them who genuinely cares. The David versus Goliath narrative is powerful, and will sustain and inspire, but it is not complete. The market and the state have inextricably entered their lives. It will need a caring partnership between the Dongria Kond, civil society organisations and the government to figure out how to navigate the very difficult terrain they face ahead of them, and for them to continue inspiring and teaching the rest of the world how to live lives finely tuned to nature.[9]
>
> (Kothari, 2015)

Though one does not understand as to why the Dongria Kond narrative, on its own, even as a stand-alone, could not be allowed to remain that stand-alone narrative, without the patronising approach by 'civil society' (a term that nobody even questions) and others?

(iii.) Let me move to East Godavari district in the present state of Andhra Pradesh and a road story, the third narrative.

> Few roads, like the road to Kondamodalu[10], cruise so perfectly through life's close hits and misses. If you fall ill in Kondamodalu, the minimum price to pay for life is a three-hour boat ride on the Godavari – survival

not guaranteed during the monsoons with the Godavari in turbulence. Sometimes, children have been delivered mid-way, unable to wait till they arrived at the hospital hours away ...[11] For, nothing but a myth of a road exists between Kondamodalu and the nearest government hospital. It may take lesser time to reach a doctor far away, or bring the doctors closer ... The distance between life and death on the road to Kondamodalu, is the distance between the myth and reality of "beneficiaries" of democracy. The road to Kondamodalu is both a metaphor and a reality; or, one where metaphor and reality of a state and its systems converge. It marks an almost imperceptible distance between relief and rehabilitation and displacement. The pathos unleashed by the "2006 Godavari"[12] lay in the fact that, at least for the 12 out of 14 villages of Kondamodalu panchayat, the road to Kondamodalu was the only alternative source of surviving it ... 2006 Godavari will be an important turning point in the official response to floods. And a sheer paradox. For now, these "Godavari affected families" have turned into daily wage-earners building their own road towards their own displacement. Making it convenient for the government to smoothen out at least one rough feather in the long battle to build the Polavaram dam.[13] Kondamodalu has a population of 1,960 ST families (approximately), with one Primary Health Care Centre for 14 villages and an apology for a road, among other handicaps. The way to reach people in normal times is through the far simpler and more beautiful Godavari on everyday launches. But during monsoons most of this part is out of access. Since years, this has been the case ... The road to Kondamodalu starts from a point near Rampachodavaram, and is a near-about 35 kilometers long stretch of a "kuccha" road, inlaid with boulders and stones and passing through streams of water at intervals. And a pristine forest with (older) Rosewood and (younger) Teak trees, among other local species ... For ... two decades (or more) people of Kondamodalu panchayat have been requesting the ITDA to repair the road [to no avail] ... [But] on 11th August, passing through this road, one realised ... it was literally the case of "build, or perish". For accessing the relief rightfully their due, the men and women of flooded Kondamodalu village panchayat were employed by the ITDA. People from Somalapadu, Kokarigudem, Kathanapally [were] working on it ... Accompanying me that evening at 7 pm, on the way back from Kondamodalu, were five young men [from these] and other villages. They had come to the forest clearing to collect food which was air-dropped hours ago. The jeep [I had hired], they surmised, would take them closest to the point from where they could walk back to their respective villages. Woefully for them, they ended up walking me down to Kakavada since the jeep refused to budge after the mishap – almost pushing us deep down into the valley. We walked from 7 pm that evening to 4 am the next morning through intermittent downpour. For those men, it meant paying a price ... Having to walk back a day later to their homes, all for a loaf of bread, literally and figuratively...The walk from Kondamodalu that night made me realise...if there was no road until then, it was because these were tribes with "survival instincts"[14]. And if there was going to be a road now, after all, it was to push them into fringes of existence through their own labour! ... And it is easier to move the "flood-affected" rather than the "dam-affected". Government, NGOs and media either did not reach them or were unable to...Food, water, basic needs had failed to reach them ...'

(Umamaheshwari, 2014: 82–4)

I met the ITDA PO Murali in 2006 at Rampachodavaram, who happened to be the administrator of the R&R component of the Polavaram project. He said,

'The Polavaram project occupies 70 per cent of our time.'

(Umamaheshwari, 2014: 79)

'Integrated tribal development' has been, in the Polavaram case, integrated tribal displacement. I had met him when Godavari had come in spate (a few days after that coming) when he enlightened me about two categories that I found rather funny and sad at the same time. 'GAF's and 'PAF's (he literally said that – only when I asked him did he clarify what they meant). He said, 'The Polavaram project will be like rehabilitating GAFs (Godavari Affected families). Anyhow they will get affected. Survey of PAF (Project affected families) is happening.' For him it was just a matter of an altered acronym. He then said, 'By the way, the list (of households) prepared for Polavaram project came in handy for relief. It was easy for teams to distribute rice and kerosene.' So, did it mean ITDA did not have the list prior to this? Or that the List was prepared only for dislocating people for Polavaram?

(Ibid, 2014: 80)

In the human project (not the human condition), in the postcolonial discourse then, there are lists and acronyms, which distance and necessarily construct a gaze from the above and the outside.

About the road, he said,

There was a sanction for the 30 km road between Lankapaka to Kondamodalu. Since these villages (Kondamodalu) will get submerged under Polavaram, they [the government] diverted the money. But I revived the proposal ... I have given them my own reasoning for it. I said if these villages get submerged, anyways we will have to transport people, shift animals etc from there. The project will anyways take three to five years to complete, At least people can use that road and it will be comfortable for the administration as well. We are laying the road under Food for Work programme...There are some very precious trees in these forests...These are smuggled by the tribals. When they drag these trees on these roads they get damaged...Tribal people are mostly encroaching on government land...In order to include them in revenue records we carried out an 'enjoyment survey' of patta and government lands. If it is not objectionable to us we will give pattas. And then compensate land for land. In a way, Polavaram project is a great opportunity for tribal families affected by floods on a permanent basis.

(Ibid: 79–80)

The backdrop, defining 'oustees', etc.

The entry point, speaking of locating oneself, is the perception of injustice *without*; and it is based on listening-in to people in the submergence zone of the Indira Sagar (Polavaram) National project in Andhra Pradesh (which was bifurcated in the year 2013 to create the Telangana State) over Godavari river. It will displace more than 300,000 people and submerge more than 276 villages in AP-Telangana alone, besides villages in two panchayats each of Odisha and Chhattisgarh states (which have filed cases against AP on the issue). The multi-purpose project promises 960 MW electricity and water essentially for the APPCPIR (Andhra Pradesh Petroleum and Petrochemicals Investment Region) with investments from private companies (including MNCs) such as Reliance and Cairn Energy and for Special Economic Zones (SEZs) on the south-east coastal industrial corridor (and its residuals for people in the cities, including Vizag) by wiping out sites of histories, memories, cultures and even concepts of citizenship of over three lakh people, most of them STs and others being the more vulnerable SCs and OBCs (riverine fisher communities). What I speak comes from learning from the people, to be displaced, the extreme ironies of, or let us say, the overturning of every idea of justice that one had truly (personally speaking) assumed was safe in our Constitution. There is an entire world and an entire history that is revealed of only injustices suffered by these communities, with only the names and designations of perpetrators varying from the non-tribal upper caste landlord to a corrupt RDO, to a wily NGO director by the day and state agent by the night. The displaced, 'internally displaced', 'oustees' are basically 'sites' to be governed, administered through jurisprudence and Constitutional provisions. The system has already designated a place for an 'oustee' even if 'inclusion' has yet not happened for most.

As quantified by the United Nations, the number of people subject to scenarios of displacement is vast – 1 in every 297 persons on this planet, including a new category officially recognised by the UN, the internally displaced person (IDP), who is forced from home but not region or country. There are at least 25 million refugees, the population equivalent to double the world's largest metropolis.

(Gans, Jelacic, 2003: 119)

'Oustees' are constantly being made once every few years, constantly ending up as names and files in litigations, for justice, with the state or other authorities. The term 'oustee', incidentally, is defined in one of the classic long-drawn displacement battle – the Narmada Sardar Sarovar Project – in the 'Narmada Water Dispute Tribunal Award on R&R' thus:

> An oustee shall mean any person who since at least one year prior to the date of publication of the notification under Section-4 of the Act, has been ordinarily residing or cultivating land or carrying on any trade, occupation or calling or working for gain in the area likely to be submerged permanently or temporarily.

In the Indian context,

> It is estimated that dams are the biggest causes of displacement in the country, although actual figures regarding the number of people displaced range from 20 to 50 million. However, it is generally agreed that about 40 per cent of those displaced belong to the Scheduled Tribes.[15]
>
> (Xaxa Committee Report, 2014: 49)

Incidentally, the Scheduled Tribes constitute 8.6 per cent of the total population (2011 census). According to various estimates in the last few years, 52 per cent of tribal people are displaced by mines, 75 per cent by wildlife sanctuaries and 38 per cent by dams. Only 25 per cent of those displaced by development projects has been rehabilitated. Speaking of the experience of communities displaced from dam projects in the past, Smithu Kothari writes:

> 25 years after the building of the prestigious Bhakra-Nangal project, only 730 of the 2,108 families displaced in the early 1950s from the Bilaspur and Una districts of Himachal Pradesh, had been resettled. A majority of those displaced by other renowned projects, like the Hirakud dam in Orissa or the Rihand dam in Uttar Pradesh, have never been officially resettled. The other illustrative example is that of the oustees of the Pong dam in Himachal Pradesh, who were displaced in the late 1960s. Out of the 30,000 families or more that were displaced, only 16,000 were found eligible for compensation and in the end only 3,756 were moved hundreds of miles to a completely different cultural, linguistic and ecological zone in Rajasthan. Some of the land meant for their occupation was already occupied, while most of the other land was uncultivable. Compounding this, the host community was not prepared for their arrival and eventually over 75 per cent turned to Himachal only to find minimal support for their re-establishment. They migrated all over the northern part of the country, most of them in various stages of destitution.
>
> (Kothari, 1996: 1479)

The displaced here are people whose Selfs have had several Selfs constructed for them: a Self from the outside as to who this Tribal Self, as in *persona*, is – the government-constructed one, the NGO-constructed one (changing as per definitions changing on the basis of global political economy and *where* the charity is being bid for, and towards *which* project, at which moment in contemporary time); forester-constructed one; the development-jargon constructed Self and so on. There are multiple contexts; there is an image, and there is a constructed image (both are not the same), much like in photography and in colonial anthropology and in lab-science.

Prof. Gopal Guru[16] had mentioned a criterion: that of feeling, when people feel that injustice has been done, as being the starting point. In this case, then, the communities have not just 'felt' the injustices but also raised battle cries every once too often, and thus they have a legitimate right to be heard and acknowledged. The Polavaram, in any case, seems to appear as a battle lost or a lost cause by now, with N. Chandrababu Naidu (CM of AP) promising a Singaporean capital and K. Chandrasekhara Rao (CM of Telangana) promising a Shanghai (or whatever) – each side having put a stamp on the destruction to be unleashed on the forests, land and river of Godavari-Sabari region, having played with every Constitutional guarantee ensured on paper, in other words, ensured injustice through systems of justice. But it is amazing to find these communities still fighting their cases in courts and still making pleas through petitions and protests, with an innate sense of some 'justice out there' that will reach them. There was, once, the state, and there was the market; but what happens when the state becomes market and market becomes state?

Noam Chomsky makes a point about the contemporary state of affairs thus:

> The nature of the system is that it's supposed to be driven by greed; no one's supposed to be concerned for anybody else, nobody's supposed to worry about the common good – those are not things that are supposed to motivate you, that's the principle of the system. The theory is that private vices lead to public benefits – that's what they teach you in economics departments …
>
> (Peter Mitchel, 2002: 62)

Further,

> What's been happening in the contemporary period is really something quite new in history, actually. I mean, in recent years a completely new form of government is being pioneered, one designed to serve the developing needs of this new international corporate ruling class – it's what has sometimes been called an emerging 'de facto world government.' That's what all of the new international trade agreements are about … It's increasingly taking shape in international financial organisations like

the International Monetary Fund, the World Bank, the Inter-American Development Bank, the World Trade Organisation, the G-7 planning meetings of the rich industrial countries...These are all efforts to try to centralise power in a world economic system geared towards ensuring that 'policy is insulated from politics' ... The World Bank has its own term for the phenomenon: they call it 'technocratic insulation.' So if you read World Bank studies, they talk about the importance of having 'technocratic insulation' – meaning a bunch of technocrats, who are essentially employees of the big transnational corporations, have to be working somewhere in 'insulation' from the public to design all the policies, because if the public ever gets involved in the process they may have bad ideas, like wanting the kind of economic growth that does things for people instead of profits, all sorts of stupid stuff like that. So therefore what you want to have is insulated technocrats – and once they're insulated enough, then you can have all the 'democracy' you like, since it's not going to make any difference. In the international business press, this has all been described pretty frankly as 'The New Imperial Age'.

(Ibid: 381)

One may perhaps add here that this kind of 'insulation' is not simply of technocrats but also increasingly of the mainstream, urban-based media and the larger academic fraternity as well whose wages have shown higher growth rate in the last decade than ever before, post-independence, which may be just one kind of insulation from the hard facts of dislocation, distress and poverty faced by the majority. In this 'new age' (whether or not it refers back to Imperialism of the West) then,

Neither foreign powers seeking control over natural resources nor foreign companies in a 'cash crop' production like sneakers have tended to invest in the infrastructure or future of their host nation, with the consequence of underdevelopment and displacement more often than the showcase success of towns like Hyderabad, India. One typical pattern of migration in relation to investment begins with the move of subsistence farmers to the local city in pursuit of the new jobs, and then to the world city-at-large when the jobs disappear as foreign investment moves on. The accrued mass of individual movement has large consequences, such as the reduced agricultural production and environmental degradation of abandoned land and the overstressed physical and social infrastructure of rapidly expanding cities ... In its drive to expand and its ability to do so without sovereign limits, capital spurs these related human displacements: deruralisation, migration, emigration and flight.

(Gans, Jelacic, 2003: 119)

When the nature of state has radically transformed, how do you, or *do you*, approach the same state for justice for people they have *by design* marginalised and kept marginal, only to dole out charity to them from time to time? So, does the theory of justice and its adequacy also need to get tested against the changing role and form and content of the state, a market-state? For when state becomes invisible, it is far more dangerous than when the state is visible and interventionist. State is there, and not there, so to speak; there to impose itself, arrest, punish, but not there when people want it to intervene, especially some people who want it to intervene for rendering them justice.

Verticality of/in the system

Though seemingly unconnected, I want to point to one of the idioms of our times – tall apartment complexes. Or *an* example of our times – the Antilla@ Mumbai[17] – whose background story (which is its own 'India' story, as well) as well as design (it is quite politically ingrained architecture, which needs to be seen as such) goes from the ground to the top, skywards in one linear from; it is a story that moves upwards; it is absolutely vertical. In this *verticality*, then, some languages are used and some languages are not used at all; gradients, here, are not allowed and no curves either, unless at the end they peak-up to a straight line pointing skywards: a straight line, right up to the ambition or aspiration or the false promise of the 10 per cent GDP (which could also be, inversely, a General Displacement Project). The American economy was built thus, vertically, with skyscrapers being the idea of the American 'dream'. What would be the view from these skyscrapers? What would it show? Is there a horizontal spatial paradigm which can include? In this *verticality*, the possibility of spatial expansiveness, that could include, seems impossible. From the top, the view is always of a far distant ground below; the higher you go, the smaller (or more insignificant) the things on the ground appear. And what lies at the other end of this spatial canvas? The view from the ground must necessarily be about looking up, either in aspiration, or with sheer resentment, or with slow anger or dejection welling up within as to why the distance between the ground and the highest level is so vast. Incidentally, the vertically oriented 'smart city' has needs evaluated for next 15 years of water, electricity, power and so on, whereas the needs of a rural area, of Scheduled Tribes and Scheduled Castes, are evaluated on a five-year basis and change with every presentation of a new budget. Smart cities are supposedly future-looking; non-'smart' villages are redundant and shall remain inconsequential to the present economic politics or political economics. Can there be an adequate theory not yet born, that might define justice within such a vertical paradigm?

Paradoxes

The 2011 Global Hunger Index (GHI) Report ranked India 15th, among the leading countries in hunger situation. The Oxford Poverty and Human

Development Initiative using a Multi-dimensional Poverty Index (MPI) reports that there are 645 million poor living under the MPI in India. This number is higher than the 410 million poor living in the 26 poorest African nations. Official estimates vary, but it is generally believed that India has roughly about 60 million poor households, accounting for over 350 million people, about 35 per cent of the entire population. What is the other side of the India story? The combined wealth of India's richest 100 people was $241 billion in 2011, according to the Forbes India Rich List, which includes 57 Dollar Billionaires. Nita Ambani's[18] birthday gift: an Airbus 319 Corporate Jet costing Rs. 242 crores. As of the year 2013, the Hindi cinema star, Shah Rukh Khan made Rs. 220.5 crores through films and endorsements. Katrina Kaif, the Hindi film actress, made Rs. 63.75 crores through films and endorsements. The Indian cricket player (who was captain of the Indian cricket team until recently) M.S. Dhoni became the 23rd in the Forbes Rich List not long ago, with a net-worth of US$ 31 million. Many are added to the list of aspirants at regular intervals – sportspersons, mainstream English fiction writers, fashion designers, etc.

The Rich List is fairly inclusive while the 'oustees' list is an exclusive domain – of the excluded; they are 'valued' at the minimum daily wage of Rs. 150 per day per person. The reasons for producing Dollar Billionaires are intricately linked to the reasons for a majority of the population fighting for survival amidst poverty and uprooted from socio-cultural contexts once too often. One section's progress has necessarily come to mean another's deprivation. Development should have ideally been de-linked from displacement. What should have been, for the largest number of people, an enriching alternative to improve lives and choices, has ended up with a few Dollar Billionaires pitched against the rest, with the state functioning more as their protector, acquiring land and other resources for their profit. But when the term 'development' itself has assumed a new meaning in the economic dictionary (where even land brokers and contractors are called 'developers' and 'infrastructure development' has assumed the meaning of real-estate development), we cannot expect much. Strangely enough, in spite of the number of welfare-oriented schemes of the government (in rural areas, such as the rural employment guarantee scheme, the MGNREG), we do not find any decrease in the number of newer poorer migrants to urban areas, and increasing number of homeless, living on alms, and increasingly, with decapitated arms or legs. The state of the physical torture they put themselves through in order to survive is surely meant, at the face value, to cause severe guilt among those better-off, but its inner symbolism digs deep into the dichotomy of bare survival and greed; abject hunger and sheer gluttony.

Stiglitz wrote that

> Globalisation proves that change does not invariably produce progress. In America we have also seen change, and seemingly at an ever

faster pace – but here, too, it is not clear if most Americans are better off. Recent numbers suggest that productivity growth is increasing at the impressive speed of over 4 percent per annum. Americans who work are working longer hours, while more and more Americans are not working: some are openly unemployed; some are so discouraged by the lack of jobs that they have stopped looking (and therefore are no longer included in the unemployment statistics) ... Many are concerned, moreover, by the seeming erosion of moral values exhibited so strikingly in the corporate scandals that rocked the country in the last few years ... This seeming erosion of moral values is just one change (the increasing bleakness of the suburban landscape in which so many Americans live is another) that does not seem to indicate progress.

(Stiglitz, 2004: 18–19)

The erstwhile Planning Commission's 11th Five Year Plan document[19] had noted that, 'In the Tenth Plan period (2002–03 to 2006–07) the economy accelerated to record an average growth of 7.7%, per annum. The growth rate in the last four years of the Plan has averaged 8.7%, making India one of the fastest growing economies in the world.' At the same time, it acknowledged that 'National Family Health Survey-3 (NFHS-3) shows that almost 46% of the children in the 0 to 3 years' age group suffered from malnutrition in 2005–06'. It has also been noted that between 1995 and 2010 over a quarter of a million farmers' suicides were reported. Very clearly, high economic growth did nothing to the levels of distress or poverty of the largest mass. Yet, the 11th FYP sought a different remedy for this ailment, namely

Growth in the Eleventh Plan should be better balanced to rapidly create jobs in the industrial and services sectors. This is necessary if a significant portion of the labour force is to shift out of agriculture, where it is currently engaged in low productivity employment, into a non-agricultural activity that can provide higher real incomes per head.

However, if we went back into history, the Planning Commission, set up in March 1950 by a Resolution of the Government of India, had a different scope of work altogether, namely

The Constitution of India has guaranteed certain Fundamental Rights to the citizens of India and enunciated certain Directive Principles of State Policy, that the State shall strive to promote the welfare of the people by securing and protecting as effectively as it may a social order in which justice, social, economic and political, shall inform all the institutions of the national life, and shall direct its policy towards securing, among other things: a. that the citizens, men and women equally, have the right to an adequate means of livelihood; b. that the ownership and control of the material resources of the community are so distributed as best to subserve the common good; and c. that the operation of the economic system does not result in the concentration of wealth and means of production to the common detriment.[20]

Surely, these have remained mere lofty ideals that look good on paper. The present is a moment of constructed disconnect and distance between the state and the mass of disadvantaged people who are increasingly being dealt with in a patronising and paternalising tone. At the other end, the historical-geographic location of tribal communities in India brings them directly in line of the massive expansion of global extractive capitalist interests. The Xaxa Committee Report states, for instance, that:

> With regard to mineral resources, three States with substantial tribal populations – Odisha, Chhattisgarh and Jharkhand – have considerable mineral reserves. These three States alone account for 70 per cent of India's coal reserves, 80 per cent of its high-grade iron ore, 60 per cent of its bauxite and almost 100 per cent of its chromite reserves. Indeed, according to the Centre for Science and Environment, about half of the top mineral-producing districts are tribal districts – and these are also districts with forest cover of 28 per cent which is larger than the national average of 20.9 per cent. Unfortunately, much of this forest land has been diverted for mining purposes resulting in environmental degradation, loss of livelihood, and displacement of tribal communities. Many of these mineral-bearing areas are also affected by the on-going conflict between the Maoists and the State.
>
> (Xaxa Committee Report, 2014: 49)

The same goes for their location within forests, wherein 51 out of 58 districts in India with more than 67 per cent forest cover are tribal districts (Ibid: 49). But here, too, they have to bear the brunt of the colonial forestry rules and be deemed 'encroachers' on their own land, especially in wildlife sanctuaries, national parks and protected areas, with little concession that came in the form of FRA, where again the onus on proving their *podu* patches is on the communities and if these come within National Parks, the FRA becomes almost inconsequential. The *system* also comes up with ever-new ways of configuring even environment and landscapes in order to maximise monetary profit. For instance, in a recently released High Level Committee report on the various Acts of the Ministry of Environment, Forests and Climate Change (MOEFCC), Government of India,[21] there is seen an effort to re-define 'Forest'. In a situation where FRA Act has been put in place, to expand the notion of access of tribal communities to their forest-land and also giving recognition to traditions such as *podu* (shifting cultivation or slash-and-burn) they practise, a redefinition of Forest might bring in more ambiguities while administering justice to these communities in the event of displacement. And bringing in private players into the picture (not that it had not happened before).

For its part, the TSR Committee report acknowledges the fact (though uncritically) that

> The proportion of Indians living in cities increased to 360 million in 2011, making a quantum jump from 62 million in 19517. In independent India's quest for development, total power generation has jumped from 6.6 billion KWH in '50s reaching to a current level of 961 billion KWH; large segments of the country still have pathetically inadequate, irregular power supply, to meet even current requirements ... Domestic consumption of petroleum products increased from 3.3 million tonne in 1951 to 158.2 million tonnes in 2012–13.
>
> (HLC Report, 2014: 21)

And that

> With 2.3% of the world's land area, India accounts for 7.8% of recorded species. It has 668 protected areas, 15 biosphere reserves and 26 Ramsar Convention sites. There are four biodiversity hotspots; the Western and Eastern Himalayas, North East India, parts of the Western Ghats and Nicobar. In addition there are other areas of rich biological diversity along parts of the coastline and elsewhere.
>
> (Ibid: 29)

But it issues a caveat

> It is the view of the Committee that areas which are rich in biodiversity must be strongly protected and activity allowed in these areas *only when there is an overwhelming advantage in terms of economic development* ... It should be made clear that no activity will be permitted which threatens the environment and biodiversity of these areas. *This will exclude such areas from expressions of interest by user agencies (UA) thus saving valuable time and litigation. There will however be one exception. Where there are considerations of national interest and issues relating to safeguarding the territorial integrity of the country, activities may be permitted in such areas subject to the prior and specific approval of the union Cabinet.*
>
> (Ibid. Emphasis mine)

So, 'activities' may be allowed within forest areas, even in bio-diversity rich and Ramsar sites, if the state perceives possibility of 'economic development' – a vague term and 'national interest'. These two terminologies – national interest and economic development – can subsume all else, including rights of forest-dwelling and forest-based communities as well as the ecological life (comprising wildlife, and several imperceptible living organisms within) of a forest, not to forget its intangible, non-economic value for communities.

Understanding life: a different knowledge system, and self

The Kondareddis follow a system of storing grain which is community owned, cultivated in lands that were for very long owned communally, and this grain bank fed members of the community who could not for any reason be agriculturally productive for a particular season. Their family was fed by the stocks preserved for these exigencies. If this system seems 'backward' and 'primitive', it is better that way, since it addresses some real concerns of justice and protection of the weaker by the entire community and seeing that nobody suffers from want of any nature. It is true as it was shared by a Kondareddi woman, Vijaya once that they have never known starvation in those villages, which, in the government's lens, and its idea of justice, seems backward and needs to accept the compensation for a 'better life'. The problem is one of knowledge systems: the imposition of one universalised knowledge system over a general or generic citizenry within which notions of justice will be experimented, making it imperative to understand justice from within a centralised legal apparatus that exists to give the modern postcolonial nation a sense of its significance and its necessity to keep the world going, which is a large and over-growing middle class where caste, tribe and other social identities seem blurred but get reinstated. If justice extends to one section, the other is deprived of it, by its very nature justice cannot be a universal category because it works within parameters of judgments and judgement is itself a closed term: it 'judges'. And hence has to be once or twice removed from the matter being judged or the person or the concept being judged. It is not an 'engaged position' and certainly not from the location of the displaced and their spaces which are to be given over for an R&R package that comes, supposedly, from an idea of 'justice' but inversely from the belief that some communities' histories and historical agency can be sacrificed for a 'larger public good'. Loss of historical roots is a far deeper and dangerous problem than has been adequately discussed in any talk of social justice.

In almost all cases, displacements occur and have been occurring alongside deeper ecological impacts, and in nearly all cases, tribal communities or indigenous peoples have been at the heart of these. So in many ways concerns of justice in the context of displacements are concerns of environmental, social and political justice of the most marginalised who happen to reside in the most mineral-rich belts without having seen these mineral reserves in economic or currency terms (so, for sale), and as a result these sites are the most fiercely contested sites in the world where issues of indigenous or adivasi or tribal communities (as also other dalits in close proximity to them) and global political economy converge, and hence justice as an idea in these situations must come from an intense engagement with politics of market fundamentalism or expansionism, as well as politics that constructs the adivasi or tribal communities as the system's permanent, perpetual 'other', weaker and to be meddled with, through state policy in ways that gives them no choice but to be dismembered from the bodypolitik of the state or nation. The ecological sites are equally historical and also political sites for communities such as the Dongria Konds, Kondareddis, Koyas and so on. For fishermen, the river is a historical-social and political site as well, something they have interacted with and preserved also as sites of their identity. The issue of displacement, in the case of Polavaram dam, is deeply connected with the issue of irreversible ecological damage (as was the case with most of the mining and dam building projects) and any effort at theory of justice would have to address both the concerns of justice as a generic and environmental justice as being one where the needs of the most marginalised (in democracy) are seen not merely as 'livelihood needs' but also as their just and rightful claim to their historic and political being, in a location, not as a permanent beneficiary of the state. Today's neo-liberal economic regime is one that is deeply linked to environmental geo-politics.

In the course of journeys in the Godavari region in the context of displacement from the Indira Sagar dam, I had met Madi Muttem, a Kondareddi woman from Kokkarigudem in Kondamodalu in East Godavari District of the then unified Andhra Pradesh (when she spoke to me) now in the new state of Andhra Pradesh.

> I am the MPTC[22] (member) for two mandals – Kondamodalu and Tunnur My name is Madi Muttamma. We cannot survive in plain area[23]; this is *Agency*, and hence we have all things we need; in the town in a plain area you have to *buy* everything – vegetables, edible leaves, fruits, tamarind, etc. *Here*, in the agency, we get all of those for *free*. We just need to buy salt, which we get from our village *santa* (the weekly village fairs). *There*, we cannot survive. They say they will build our homes in places which we shall show them; they have not yet shown us anything yet …[24]

Her home lies within the submergence zone of the Polavaram dam and what she had said to me then addressed all the three sites: self, home and habitat. These sites are, at once, personal, political and historically rooted. And the *in-construction* sites that she speaks about are the Submergence Zone as a site, village as a site and an economic construct as a site. So, her Self and her idea of who she is, her *I*, or *we*, so to speak, are located within all these sites and each of these together creates the discourse on autonomy and Self of the tribal person/adivasi.

Destroying this dynamic sense of Self and autonomy (all over again; the last one happened during the British colonial regime) will be the Polavaram dam (multi-purpose) National project here. It will destruct the lives of 300,000 (or more) people, nearly 80 per cent of them adivasi/tribal communities of Koya, Kondareddi, Konda Kammaras, Konda Valmikis, Naikpods and other dalits, including fisher communities settled around and along the river Godavari. The earliest revolts by these communities are recorded in the colonial records from the 19th century, and there may have been others before the colonial times, of which not much-recorded history is available to us, as of now. That the dam will dislocate and dispossess these communities is one part of the story; that it will do so, in order to give the globally linked and globally oriented industries (from India and abroad – Reliance, Pharmocell, Cairn Energy, among others) most of the 960 MW portion of the electricity, and its residuals to people like us in the cities and in universities and other institutions, is another part of the story. In the midst of this, Madi Muttem's was a simple, deep and profound understanding of the *akkada (There)* and *ikkada (Here)*. The concept of *ikkada* (here) versus *akkada* (there) was the most reflective philosophical point which nearly all the tribal women spoke to me about in the submergence zone. *Ikkada* and *akkada* would occur in a context of contrasts (of being the adivasi person rooted in a historical location versus becoming a state and market project, or in other words, the sacrificial goat for the bogey of public good).

> *Akkada*, or *There*, is a nameless, disempowering, vague, abstract notion of a place they will be 'thrown into' (*padestaaru – they will throw us*, said many, so they felt they were perceived as things that can be thrown into someplace) and following from there, they will lose their identities and livelihoods. Even if they happened to know the name of the 'RR colony' (in two cases in Polavaram mandal) it was always referred to as 'there', 'that place' (vague, abstract, nameless); no matter how difficult lives were 'here' (their homes by the tamarind and toddy and the forested hills) – it is still their home ...
>
> (Umamaheshwari, R. 2014: 17–18)

This is the *ikkada* they would rather live and die in. One of the Kondareddi men, perhaps it was Gangaraju or was it Ranga Reddi (?), said to me, the town has always been within reach for us, nobody stopped us from going there and settling down, but we live Here, by choice, this is home.

> The 'here' and 'there' are two poles – between their own ('my own') and 'that' which does not belong to them or where they do not belong but will be dumped at. Incidentally, the government machinery had the same language – '*ikkada meeru em chestaaru, adavillo undi? Akkada meeku anni sadupayalu untaayi*' ('what will you do Here, staying in forests? *There* you will get all facilities').
>
> (Ibid: 18)

The state's perception of 'here' – as I heard over and over again in the officials' propaganda for the Polavaram project – could be a chapter right out of the enlightenment rationality project where the adivasis were indeed 'savages' that needed to be 'civilised' and hence the 'there' was that 'civilising' mission. On the other hand, for the people, the 'here' was their historically located site which was a labour of their own love and preservation over several generations. The 'Self' of the tribal woman or man or child has not been an autonomous entity (by itself) ever since the colonial rulers set foot on their territories in India. The Tribal Self has been constructed through the language of several others – essentialised, and thence, worked upon. There is politics to the making of this Self – definition, and histories, years of being either in control of or being driven to subservience makes these Selves; and there is a Self that others construct for you – to tell you who you are; who they are, who the others we see from the outside are. And these constructions come from the politics of those who construct, based on biases, perceptions, and perspectives. The Self of the tribal person so far created has resulted, mostly, almost universally in their context, to creating an *I* or the Self with far less self-esteem than they had in the pasts of their resistances, the memory of which only exists in the records of the English colonisers or in community memory. The debilitating poverty of the tribal person without the cognition of this located Self, I have seen, also ends in amnesia about their pasts, and keeps them away from autonomy. This may be true for minorities and landless dalits in other contexts as well. What is remembered is vectored through the present state of being.

> When it arises, the self begins to speak of itself grandiloquently as subject, as individual mind, self, or ego, the center or agent of consciousness, and, in so doing, not only radically alters the vocabulary of political theory but also fundamentally changes our perception of political things.
>
> (Zetterbaum, 1982: 59)

The point of arising, incidentally, is dependent on the present location. They say that colonisation destroyed some thousand languages spoken by the indigenous Americans; language should be understood as more than just a speech category. The language within which they engaged with the world around them – in ideas of nature, earth and a sense of larger connection with the universe as a cycle, was destroyed through a long process. In India, too, several indigenous people have lost their language and thence, history, to a kind of literacy-oriented world (I say kind of, so that we understand that even non-alphabetical scripts may exist or have existed without being granted the status of a script). Self-definition makes a political statement, only so far as it comes from within. When it becomes a chain, or essential category for state, or the development project, problems arise.

The adivasi person is, in effect, a non-person, and only retrievable or retrieved as part of a whole and not an entire whole in herself or himself. Hence the essentialising projects usually treat the individual similarly, as collective subjects that need intervention to make sense of who they are, as a community within the larger canvas. Autonomy as an individual is only available for the middle classes or the elite whose sense of privacy, personal space, is distinguishable quite clinically from the public. And even in the 'public spaces' their 'private' or privacy is meant to be protected. In the context of women's rights in public spaces this discourse is predominant. But these rights are not available to women of the adivasi groups, who are still seen in collective terms and sometimes as beings whose *Selves* have not yet evolved to that level that they may claim personal space or privacy as right in matters where their entire homes have been dislocated by the state. They remain collectives in whose interest representations are made by activists or political groups in the name of giving them equitable compensation for collective homes (not individual homes which may reflect an individual woman's own self, her creativity or her idea of space, distinct from the other tribal woman's home) of collective, non-persona based names (usually without faces attached to these names, without histories) razed to the ground for a project that claims to be for an equally vague collective/public 'good', decided by the state acting supposedly in the interest of the people of the nation (again, comprising of non-problematic or unqualified numbers, with names but no individual historic faces) while protection, in an ideal world, should have been about allowing for the full expression of Self in a context where the historical, cultural, political Self has gained acknowledgement. But *which* Self ultimately gets protection by the state in today's context? It is an essentialised category called 'tribe' (with an alter-name called 'adivasi' but within similar essentialist structures of discourse) with a name and a colonial project-based face which fixes the community or the person to a certain space and considers this enough to guarantee some protections in a constitutional document without bothering to even implement that fully. And in this protection of an anthropological project called tribe, the nature of intervention through tools of modernity does not allow space for a Self with a purpose of self-fulfilment based on a different idea that goes against the idea of the state as to what is development and what is needed to 'civilise' the tribe. There is no Self, but fixing of names and categories, in the understanding of post-colonial state of adivasi.

Missing in the present mainstream understanding (of R&R under a kind of assumed system of justice) is the significance of history and memory of the people displaced; history and memory never gained their due place in conceptions of justice, especially when it concerns those that have been rendered marginalised by that very fact of denial of their history and memory and an imposition of a common identity over them as 'beneficiaries', 'oustees', refugees, etc. Displacement of human beings is seen as adequately 'compensation-able' in modern political theories of state and governance. Where the term 'R&R' has come to be understood as a 'Right' in an assumed sense of 'fair-play' by the modern democratic state with several agencies – NGOs, activists, others – debating about measuring the 'adequate-ness' and 'fairness'. Usha Ramanathan rightly points out

> Compensation is seen as the means for reducing the injustice inherent in acquisition. Every law that dispossesses carries a provision for compensation which is intended to soften the blow. Yet, the limited understanding of compensation has eroded its moral base.
>
> (Ramanathan, 1996: 1488)

Re-evaluation of the term 'justice' could perhaps take reference from the Bolivian Constitution, 2009 and its embodying of the vision of nature, cultural attachment to land and territory of the indigenous people. The Bolivian Constitution, debated in a Constituent Assembly in 2006 and 2007 called by the country's first indigenous president, Evo Morales, was adopted in a referendum in January 2009. Community justice is practised with rules that are not written down but oral.

> Bolivia's indigenous cultures are based on a holistic vision of the cosmos and are intimately related to land and territory. These ethnic identity movements are rooted in communities and seek to preserve cultures that are under assault from the dominant culture and economy. First, the indigenous holistic vision of the cosmos (*cosmovisión*) asserts a unity with nature. This unifying vision guides everyday activities. Though not common to all indigenous populations, it provides a unifying element for those who maintain indigenous identity, even when living in cities and engaging in urban occupations. Second, land and territory are a focus of indigenous demands. The terms 'land' and 'territory' have different connotations, with different practical implications for the people of the highlands and of the lowlands ... Indigenous communities oppose rampant exploitation of natural resources both to protect the environment that sustains their material life and to express their unity with nature. The collective orientation of Bolivian indigenous groups is related to the cultural attachment to land and territory. Community ties are strong and the culture emphasizes community membership. They claim political representation as communities, rejecting liberal representation systems based on the individual.
>
> (Hammond, 2011: 656)

Some scholars invoke the spirit of the Indian Constitution and its provisions which aim to protect the rights of the tribal communities. For instance, Kalpana Kannabiran notes that

> The Panchayats (Extension to the Scheduled Areas) Act, 1996 (Act 40 of 1996, PESA), a legislation related to tribal governance and political autonomy is a landmark legislation ... Under PESA, the village

is construed as the habitation(s)/hamlet(s) that comprise an autoch-thonous community – a self-governing space inhabited by people with shared traditions and customs. This recognition of the 'village' as a 'living community' is vital (Sub-committee on PESA 2007:5) ... (Kannabiran, 2015: 268–9)

However, she also notes that

Alongside being offered the guarantee of autonomy and sovereignty through laws like PESA and the FRA, adivasi homelands face an acute crisis of liberty in the face of occupation by multiplicity of armed forces – state and non-state – whether in the north-east or in Chhattisgarh. A close reading of the realities of occupation – suspen-sion of public services, arbitrary arrests, torture, illegal detentions, disappearances, abduction, and an atmosphere of terror – throws up the multiple and simultaneous derogations of article 15 and article 21 rights in these regions. The roots of the routine derogation of fun-damental rights to non-discrimination and liberty lie in neo-liberal economic policy, which forces large-scale displacement and dispposses-sion of primarily indigenous tribal communities ... The intersectional interpretation of non-discrimination and liberty – which converge for this group alone in a single clause in article 15 through 'race' and 'place of birth' – holds the promise of an insurgent and transformative constitutionalism.

(Ibid: 270–71)

Back in the year 1969, at IIAS, Shimla,[25] a seminar was held and it was attended by some eminent sociologists including M.N. Srinivas. The partici-pants made some crucial observations there

The safeguards and freedom from exploitation are in relation to land alienation and land-allotment, usurious money-lending and the practice of forced and bonded labour. It is estimated that approximately 50 per cent of India's tribes depend directly or indirectly on the forests for their livelihood. Another major problem – reported to be very acute in the Central belt – is that relating to the alienation of land by tribals to non-tribals mainly to discharge debts or to obtain ready cash. From time to time legal measures have been taken by the concerned govern-ments to stop such land transfers, but due to the existence of some legal loopholes and the non-enforcement of existing legislative and executive measures the practice continues ... The Seminar felt that integration must be sharply differentiated from assimilation which means complete loss of cultural identity for the weaker groups. Each group must be able to uphold its cultural heritage with dignity and a sense of achievement.

(R.D. Sanwal, 1969: 180–1)

It is the year 2015 now.

> Koneru Ranga Rao Committee (noted that in AP state) up to 48 per cent of land is held by non-tribals in Scheduled areas, despite land transfer regulations that prohibit the transfer of lands from tribal to non-tribal sections and between non-tribals. Statistics from the Ministry of Rural Development indicate that, with respect to land that has not been alienated, close to 400,000 claims were filed for restoration of 8.5 lakh acres. Only 50 per cent of this land could be restored to adivasis ... Rampant corruption in restoration (and) litigation worsened an already difficult situation, as did the costs of travelling to frequent hearings and of sustaining such litigations, costs that further impoverished adivasi claimants ...
>
> (Kannabiran, 2015:256)

Colonialism of a certain historical vintage may have ended, but colonisation continues to happen: of ideas, histories, religion, and most important of all, economy. It is important to perceive the deeper colonising of areas purely for their resources, which have been protected and preserved by people who thought differently of the ground and the skies and the mountains and the rivers than the colonising and modernising project did. And this is a historical fact without trying to romanticise or exoticise the idea. Cultures are being destroyed and permanently displaced and marginalised peoples are being constructed everyday across the world. Several minorities are also constructed at the same time. The tribal body is a site for reinventions and reform and construction. If inclusion was such an empowering and redeeming concept, today, more than 60 years after independence we would have seen visible signs of it, but the truth is that the areas populated by communities such as Gonds, Kondareddis, Koyas, Kammaras, and several others, poverty is an imposition and getting out of the poverty web seems to exist in the only option again forced upon them which is to sell their land and take the money and leave higher things such as development of nation and high-level BRICS kinds of affairs to the others, usually, always, the non-ST, non-SC of the Constitution. And the only solace would be to have projects for the ST and SC and each project funded to give them a feeling of being included in the big game, which is actually not true. And of course, solace is supposedly to be found in the new discourse about dalit billionaires (how many are there, anyway?). In other words, there seems no way out of the paradigm of globalisation and economic growth itself, as a means and an end. Never mind if the largest land owners today in India are (after the Railways and the Army), companies like Reliance, Adani, Godrej, ITC, GMR and several like them with no connection, even remotely, with cultures called dalit or adivasi, even though they have built their empires on adivasi and dalit land. Forty per cent of those displaced by 'developmental projects' (wonder why they continue to be called so where in effect these are usually destruction projects of some kind or the other) have continued to be the Scheduled Indian 'Tribes' and there is no alternative affirmative truth emerging even in terms of these numbers reducing, even in government data. The Gonds, Kondareddis, Erukulas, Konds and Muriyas, of different regions in the country, were impoverished by the very system that essentialised them and fit them into categories of Scheduled Tribe without giving them an acceptance in the larger bodypolitik or economic integration of the kind that accepts diversity of occupation, and resources and skills. And there is non-recognition of their other identities as agriculturists, craftspersons or artisans. Kondareddis, Kammaras, Koyas, Konda Valmikis, Naikpods, Bestas and Yanadis of Godavari are today being dispossessed of their homes and memory and history.

According to identities in official records during the British colonial period metaphorically transfixed them to the positions they remained in all these years. In a sense, the transfixing and scheduling of these communities was done in an effort to quell the fierce resistance these very communities showed against the colonisers, long before the so-called Nationalist movement against British domination commenced across India. The original and very real resistance of the tribal communities was regarding their land, forests and agriculture (which was never seen as agriculture in British records, but just 'some' slash-and-burn type 'rudimentary', 'primitive' cultivation). The original movement and resistance to the British in the very basic terms of economic resistance came from the communities which, at the moment were essentialised as Scheduled Tribe, became part of the mainstream that systematically reduced them to lesser citizens, awaiting the charity of the state. The real contribution of their situation was a colonial idea of controlling their resistance movements, which had become numerous, very frequent from the 19th century (as official records would show) across the country wherever tribal communities were present. The earliest movement against colonialism came from these people, but it is only fairly recently that historians began to record and chronicle these histories. What also follows in the larger meaning of this problematic concerning all identity-based movements; does identity remain non-problematically constant and is there a singular, single identity? Sometimes, evoking of identity arises from economic contexts of deprivation. And sometimes identity is built around the nature of relationship to land and forests and river; it is not simply an identity based on the idea of descent in a reductionist sense; sometimes the village itself forms the identity and within the village the hamlet; but in official records of displacement, the village is incidental and secondary to the term 'Scheduled Tribe', in which case, the R&R is extended on a uniform basis to an 'ST' family, though from an original village, for matters of identification but not necessarily so in an R&R colony after resettlement. In government and state terms, the essentialising of tribes, as though they are permanently meant for mere sops of larger charity rather than rights as equal citizens, has tended to take the teeth out of the real and deeper resistance and struggles. It is in this context that we must locate the presence of deep state in the deepest recesses of tribal habitations today across Chhattisgarh, Andhra Pradesh, Odisha,

Maharashtra and Jharkhand, as also that of radical anti-state movements in these very locations.

Justice and environment

In justice terms, there are international conventions in place. The UN Earth Charter's principles include – respect for Earth and life in all its diversity; build democratic societies that are just, participatory, sustainable and peaceful; secure Earth's bounty and beauty for present and future generations; recognise that the freedom of action of each generation is qualified by the needs of future generations, etc. In order to keep these principles, it urges for a certain set of actions, the most important of them being – adopt patterns of production, consumption and reproduction that safeguard Earth's regenerative capacities, human rights and community well-being; eradicate poverty as an ethical, social and environmental imperative; and uphold the right of all, without discrimination, to a natural and social environment supportive of human dignity, bodily health and spiritual well-being, with special attention to the rights of indigenous peoples and minorities.[26]

There have been legal cases that have given scope for interpretation of justice based on meanings other than the assumed 'normative' which scholars have written about.

> For more than a decade, International Labor Organization (ILO) Convention 169 has specified terms under which states must recognise and protect ownership of indigenous peoples' lands and cultural practices ... The landmark ruling of the Inter American Court in The Mayagna (Sumo) Awas Tingni Community v. Nicaragua, Judgment of Aug. 31, 2001, Inter-Am. Ct. H.R. (Ser. C) No. 79 (2001), affirmed that the right to property, as articulated in article 21 of the American Convention on Human Rights, includes the communal property of indigenous people as defined by their customary use and tenure, notwithstanding its treatment under national law ... The government claimed the lands were state property because Awas Tingni members held no formal title. The court determined that applicable human rights law, including ILO Convention 169, protects indigenous peoples' land tenure such that 'possession of the land should suffice for indigenous communities lacking real title to obtain official recognition of that property.' The court ordered demarcation and titling of the Awas Tingni lands ... The court has followed and extended this approach in Moiwana Village v. Suriname, Judgment of June 15, 2005, and Yakye Axa indigenous community v. Paraguay, Judgment of June 17, 2005. In clarifying its order requiring demarcation, title, and the return of sacred territory in the latter case, the court stressed that *the valuing of indigenous lands calls for criteria other than those usually*

applicable to private property. Other considerations must be weighed because 'indigenous community culture ... derives from the relationship with traditional territories and the resources located therein, not only because these provide a means of subsistence, but because they are integral elements of their cosmovision, religion and their cultural identity.

(Willis and Seward, 2006: 18–19; Emphasis mine)

At the same time, movements worldwide over the last two decades have highlighted the global ecological impacts of economic developments across the world.

In 1991, a very dispersed and highly localised movement came together around the First National People of Colour Environmental Leadership Summit held in Washington DC. There it adopted a manifesto defining environmental justice in no less than 17 different clauses:- 'environmental justice affirms the sacredness of Mother Earth, ecological unity and interdependence of all species, and the right to be free from ecological destruction; mandates the right to ethical, balanced and responsible uses of land and renewable resources in the interest of a sustainable planet for human and other living beings ...; opposes the destructive operations of multi-national corporations ... military occupation, repression and exploitation of lands, peoples, cultures and other life forms.'

(Harvey, 1999: 157)

However, Harvey reiterates that

The abstractions cannot rest solely upon a moral politics dedicated to protecting the sanctity of Mother Earth, It has to deal in the material and institutional issues of how to organise production and distribution in general, how to confront the realities of global power politics and how to displace the hegemonic powers of capitalism not simply with dispersed, autonomous, localised, and essentially communitarian solutions...but with a rather more complex politics that recognises how environmental and social justice must be sought by a rational ordering of activities at different scales.

(Ibid: 182–4)

In conclusion, one would say that the expansive *horizontal* rather than the short-termed *verticality* of justice should also allow space for dissent and even breaking away, if need be, from what is deemed to be a covenant made between the state and the citizen-subject for showing permanent allegiance, no matter how far the state deviates from its expressed goals of protecting the interests of the citizen-subjects, whom it ought to protect, in the first place.

Notes

1 This chapter is the outcome of a seminar.
2 Though one is not so sure Mr. Ratan Tata ever travelled by an Indian train in all his life. The first meeting of Kayakalp (called the 'Innovative') Council was held on 13 May 2015 in Delhi. The other members of 'Kayakalp' Council include Mr. S.G. Mishra, General Secretary, All India Railwaymen's Federation (AIRF); Mr. M. Raghaviah, General Secretary, National Federation of Indian Railwaymen (NFIR); Ms. Ragini Yechury, Executive Director (Industrial Relations), Railway Board; and Dr. Madhukar Sinha, Executive Director (Innovation), Railway Board. Source: Press Information Bureau, Government of India (Press Release ID:121693).
3 Which means also to necessarily break away from ideas of a singular nation identity thrust upon them.
4 DP – Displaced Persons; PAPs – Project Affected Persons.
5 Directed by Christopher McLeod and co-produced by McLeod and Malinda Maynor. Released in the year 2001.
6 Source: http://nvdatabase.swarthmore.edu/content/navajo-and-hopi-tribes-cam-paign-remain-black-mesa-lands-and-protect-it-coal-mining-united-st
7 Brenda Norrell, October 5, 2009, 'A Dirty New Low for Peabody Coal', http://www.counterpunch.org/2009/10/05/a-dirty-new-low-for-peabody-coal/
8 Directed by Toby Nicholas, produced by Survival International, the film was released in the year 2009.
9 'Revisiting the legend of Niyamgiri', January 2, 2015, *The Hindu*, http://www.thehindu.com/opinion/op-ed/comment-on-niyamgiri-and-fight-between-don-gria-kondh-tribal-group-and-vedanta/article6745650.ece
10 Kondamodalu panchayat is in the East Godavari district and one of the 276 villages to be submerged under the Indira Sagar Polavaram (dam) National Project being built over the river Godavari in the state of Andhra Pradesh. The 2006 Godavari was used as an excuse by the then Y.S. Rajasekhara Reddy-ruled government in AP to get people (to be displaced by Polavaram) to sign consent letters with subject-head, *Godavari varada baadhitulu* (Godavari flood-affected people). Many people assumed they were signing to get flood-relief. Kondamodalu panchayat, at that moment, was one of the most vociferous opponents of the dam and remained blacklisted from all government schemes in normal circumstances. For a more recent and updated discussion on the present cycle of events in Kondamodalu, see R. Umamaheshwari, 'A Red Saree Bloodied Red', in *Seminar*, No. 740 (Beyond Myths: a symposium on anthropological histories of tribal worlds), April, 2021.
11 I had visited the region (then in the capacity of an independent journalist) a few days after Godavari had come in spate in the month of August, year 2006.
12 2006 Godavari is a literal translation of the way 'floods' are spoken of in this region where they call it Godavari comes and prefix the moment of the 'flood' with the year of its happening (hence, *enabhai-aaru* (or 1986) Godavari, and so on.
13 The journey that took well over 12 hours – from Kondamodalu back to Kakavada and another hour's journey to Rampachodavaram over ups and downs and rubble and slush smacked of the sheer apathy towards the Kondareddis by a system (ITDA) meant to integrate them with the mainstream.
14 Most tribal communities living by Godavari climb onto higher mountain reaches when Godavari comes and live in makeshift shelters they construct and return to their homes once the waters recede.
15 Report of the High Level Committee on Socio-Economic, Health and Educational Status of Tribal Communities of India, Ministry of Tribal Affairs, Government of India, May 2014 (Xaxa Committee Report). The Committee was headed by

sociologist, Prof. Virginius Xaxa. Other members were – Drs. Usha Ramanathan, Joseph Bara, Kamal Misra, Abhay Bang, Sunila Basant and Rusikesh Panda (Member Secretary).

16 While introducing the Seminar at IIAS, Shimla (March 2015).
17 His 27-storey house in Mumbai, which cost an estimated $1 billion.
18 Wife of Mukesh Ambani, Head of the Reliance Group of Industries, his 'net-worth' being US $22.6 billion, in the year 2011. Reliance Petrochemicals is just one of the companies invested in the completion of the Polavaram dam project.
19 Source: http://planningcommission.nic.in/plans/planrel/fiveyr/welcome.html. All the FYP documents can be downloaded from this website of the Government of India. Planning Commission is now coined Niti Ayog by the present BJP Government in power in India.
20 Ibid.
21 HLC to review various Acts administered by Ministry of Environment, Forest & Climate Change, Government of India, November 2014, headed by T.S.R Subramanian, Former Cabinet Secretary, Government of India. The Committee, incidentally, did not have a single member (other than at a bureaucratic level) engaged with issues of environment, forests-wildlife, forest-based communities and not even someone working on the issue of climate change. Other members were – Mr. Vishwanath Anand (Former Secretary to Government of India – Member); Justice (Retd.) A.K. Srivastava (Former Judge of Delhi High Court – Member); Mr. K.N. Bhat (Senior Advocate, Supreme Court of India – Member); Mr. Bishwanath Sinha (Joint Secretary, MOEFCC, Government of India – Secretary); and Mr. Hardik Shah (Member Secretary, Gujarat Pollution Control Board – Secretary).
22 Mandal Parishad Territorial Council, a unit of local self-governance in the village panchayat.
23 That is how people in the V Schedule (tribal) area refer to the non-Scheduled Areas. V Schedule area is locally referred to as Agency, a term that came in with the colonial rule. Emphasis, wherever, mine.
24 Personal communication, on 13 June 2008, at Kondamodalu.
25 Site of one's present location.
26 http://www.earthcharterinaction.org/content/pages/Read-the-Charter.html

References

Deborah Gans and Matt Jelacic, 'Displacement: The Realpolitik of Utopia', *Perspecta*, Vol. 34 (2003), pp. 118–125. Stable URL: http://www.jstor.org/stable /1567326. Accessed: 16/11/2011 02:21

David Harvey, 'The Environment of Justice', in Frank Fischer, Maarten A Hajer, Eds., *Living with Nature: Environmental Politics as Cultural Discourse*, Oxford University Press, New York, 1999, pp. 153–185.

F. Michael Willis and Timothy Seward, 'Protecting and Preserving Indigenous Communities in the Americas', *Human Rights*, Vol. 33, No. 2 (Spring 2006), pp. 18–21. Stable URL: http://www.jstor.org/stable/27880528. Accessed: 22/12/2014

John L. Hammond, 'Indigenous Community Justice in the Bolivian Constitution', *Human Rights Quarterly*, Vol. 33, No. 3, 2011, pp. 649–681. Accessed on Project Muse, DOI 10.1353/hrq.2011.0030

Joseph E. Stiglitz, 'Evaluating Economic Change', *Daedalus*, Vol. 133, No. 3, On Progress (Summer, 2004), pp. 18–25. Stable URL: http://www.jstor.org/stable /20027926. Accessed: 21/03/2011 06:51

Kalpana Kannabiran, *Tools of Justice: Non-discrimination and the Indian Constitution*, Routledge, New Delhi, 2015

Marvin Zetterbaum, 'Self and Subjectivity in Political Theory', *The Review of Politics*, Vol. 44, No. 1 (Jan., 1982), pp. 59–82, Stable URL: http://www.jstor.org/stable/1406869. Accessed: 30/12/2014 05:17

Peter R. Mitchell and John Schoeffel, eds, *Understanding Power: The Indispensable Chomsky*, The New Press, New York, 2002 (accessed at www.understandingpower.com on 7 December 2012)

R. Umamaheshwari, *When Godavari Comes: People's History of a River (Journeys in the Zone of the Dispossessed)*, Aakar Books, Delhi, 2014

R. Umamaheshwari, 'A White Saree Bloodied Red', in *Seminar*, No. 746, April, 2021.

R. D. Sanwal, 'Seminar on the Tribal Situation in India, Simla, July, 1969', *Sociological Bulletin*, Vol. 18, No. 2 (September 1969), pp. 175–181. Stable URL: http://www.jstor.org/stable/23618449. Accessed: 30/12/2014 05:18

Smitu Kothari, 'Whose Nation? The Displaced as Victims of Development', *Economic and Political Weekly*, Vol. 31, No. 24 (Jun. 15, 1996), pp. 1476–1485. Stable URL: http://www.jstor.org/stable/4404269. Accessed: 18-08-2015 10:04 UTC

Usha Ramanathan, 'Displacement and the Law', in *EPW*, Vol. 31, No. 24, 1996, pp.1486–1491.

Index

For Product Safety Concerns and Information please contact our EU
representative GPSR@taylorandfrancis.com
Taylor & Francis Verlag GmbH, Kaufingerstraße 24, 80331 München, Germany

www.ingramcontent.com/pod-product-compliance
Lightning Source LLC
Chambersburg PA
CBHW070345270326
41926CB00017B/3988